I am happy and privileged to endorse and recommend both this latest installment of Doug's publication ministry, as well as the other ministries God has birthed under Doug's leadership. Having worked in various capacities with Doug Stringer in Turning Point Ministries and Somebody Cares, I have admired his dedication to following the Lord's call, particularly in some of the more difficult, yet necessary, areas of ministry. His willingness to go where others were not willing to go has often resulted in a prophetic, clarion call to the church. After Doug and his ministries would lead out, many ministries have often been willing to follow. Many owe a debt of gratitude to Doug's simple faithfulness. This particular book gives insight into many of the principles that have motivated Doug in his obedience to God's call. Especially for those who have admired and been motivated by Doug's ministry, I believe they will find even greater encouragement as they read *Born to Die*.

Randall J. Pannell, M.Div., Ph.D.
Associate Vice President, Academic Affairs
Regent University
Virginia Beach, VA

Doug has the ability to take what is not seen as simple and make it easy to understand. I read a lot, and I have to say I'm enjoying and learning from this book as much or more than any other I've read.

Joe Kopp
Pastor, CityView Church
York, PA

This work has driven me to have a greater passion for understanding the foreshadowing of the Old Testament for today's living. This book, unlike most, will be a timeless piece of literature that should be on every Christian's shelf. This is material that will free up the church!

Richard Gibson
Business Owner and Elder,
Emmanuel Christian Fellowship
York, PA

In his new book, *Born to Die*, Dr. Doug Stringer has skillfully reminded us of those truths the apostles and early church fathers clearly understood and fervently taught, that "in the old covenant the new was concealed and in the new covenant the old is revealed." All those wonderful signs, symbols, and sacrifices were completely fulfilled in the coming, crucifixion, and resurrection of Jesus Christ. Even before reading the first line of the first chapter, Dr. Stringer had my attention in his introduction and table of contents, especially the title of Chapter 14, "The Great Exchange." There is no better way to sum up the power, purpose, and content of this book than by Doug's explanation that through the new covenant we participate in a supernatural exchange with Christ. We bring to Him what we have, no explanation necessary here, and He brings to us all that He has. This is a win-win exchange program, and we are reminded of this great Kingdom principle every time we participate in Holy Communion and we hear the minister recite the words of Christ when He raised the bread: "Take and eat; this is My body which is broken for you; do this in remembrance of Me." Then: "This cup is the new covenant in My blood. This do, as often as you drink it, in remembrance of Me." As I then backed up and read from the beginning I could only say a resounding AMEN! Thank you, Dr. Stringer, for reminding us how Christ has so fully bridged the old and new covenants.

Dr. Charles Travis
President, Logos University
Jacksonville, Florida

Doug has done a phenomenal job in unpacking the work that Jesus Christ did for us. *Born to Die* is a composite of both the Old and New Testaments knit together to form a wonderful tapestry of all that Jesus Christ did for us through His life, death, and resurrection. This book will help open the eyes of, and bring freedom to, believers and nonbelievers alike. Thank you, Doug!

Jim Herbert
Senior Pastor,
Emmanuel Christian Fellowship,
York, PA

BORN *to die*
that we may live

The Work of the Cross and the Power of the Resurrection

Doug Stringer

Bridge-Logos

Orlando, FL 32822 USA

Bridge-Logos

Orlando, FL 32822 USA

Born to Die ... That We May Live
The Work of the Cross and the Power of the Resurrection
by Doug Stringer

Copyright ©2006 by Doug Stringer

Printed in the United States of America.

Library of Congress Catalog Card Number: 2006938549
ISBN: 978-088270-338-1

Unless otherwise indicated, all Scripture quotations are from the *New King James Version* © 1979, 1980, 1982 by Thomas Nelson Publishers, Nashville, Tennessee.

Cover design by Lynette Whitesell

G163.316.N.m611.352100

DEDICATION

This book is dedicated to Bob, affectionately known as "Fergie," who was profoundly affected by this message the first time I taught it in 1993 and has been leading others to the cross ever since. Yes, Fergie, God is real, and your life and your testimony bear witness to the reality of His resurrection power at work. Keep fishing for souls, Bob! I'm proud of you and who you have become.

In Memory

In memory of Puan Sri Dato' Paduka Rosaline (Rose) Chan Yee Hing, 1952-2006, who went to be with Jesus as we were completing this book. Rose was the wife of my friend, Tan Sri (Dr.) Francis Yeoh Sock Ping, who helped inspire a portion of the chapter entitled *It Is Well With My Soul*, which is also the name of one of their favorite hymns. At the funeral, Francis said of his beloved Rose, "She ran a good race."

I have fought the good fight, I have finished the race, I have kept the faith. (2 Timothy 4:7)

ACKNOWLEDGEMENTS

I would like to gratefully acknowledge Jim Buchan for his editorial expertise, assistance, and insight along with Dr. Randall Pannell from Regent University for his theological and doctrinal review and input. Your assistance has been invaluable, as is your friendship. To my longtime friend for over 25 years, Gregory N. Carmona, for your assistance in transcribing and researching the first draft I taught in 1993. Thank you all for your faithfulness and expertise in helping communicate this important message. I also want to thank Dr. Ralph and Virginia Berkeley from Berkeley Eye Center in Houston for your comments and input when I sent you excerpts from the initial stages in the drafting of the book. Your encouragement helped me to press on!

Contents

INTRODUCTION

"God is real! God is real!"

It was 1993, and Bob had been coming to our Friday night worship services where I had been teaching an eight-week series on "The Work of the Cross." I had just completed the final message in the series, "Mission Accomplished." Bob had come to us as a skeptic, but now with tears in his eyes he came down the aisle—he came to the cross— knowing the God of the Bible is as real today as He was to the Levitical priests.

Many years later, Bob is still an integral part of our ministry. He has impacted hundreds of lives through the "Jesus in the Steps" ministry he founded along with his ministry to AIDS patients.

Who would have imagined that a study on the book of Leviticus could so profoundly change a man's life—a wrecker truck driver who for 19 years had been a hard-core heroin-methodone addict! But that is the beauty of the Word of God—from Genesis to Revelation, it never goes forth void.

This book, based on that same teaching, is not intended to be a theological treatise or an exegetical examination of the book of Leviticus. Its intent, instead, is to stir up a passion for digging deep into the Word of God, to discover the infathomable treasures of truth that lie within the pages of the Holy Scriptures. Its intent is to reveal that the God of the Scriptures—the God of ALL the Scriptures—is real!

Faith cometh by hearing, and hearing by the Word of God. (Romans 10:17)

In this world of complexities and challenges—where excellence battles with mediocrity, where vision and hope are robbed by lethargy and apathy—we need to know we are standing on the unshakable foundation of our faith, which is the Word of God. Sadly, many Christians today are faltering in their faith because of biblical illiteracy and because they lack a love for truth. I John 4 tells us how critical it is to be instructed by the Word so we may discern between the truth and error.

My desire is to provoke readers to a hunger for the Word, to delve into Scripture, to extrapolate truth, and to gleen from its perfect wisdom—not out of duty or just to find a message for a sermon, but to know and to love the very One who *IS* the treasure embedded within and entwined throughout every word, chapter, and page, which is Christ Himself.

As we watch this portrait of our Savior and the work of the cross unfold through the examination and dissection of the Levitical sacrifices, we begin to understand and share the Apostle Paul's passion to *"know Him and the power of His resurrection, and the fellowship of His sufferings..."* (Philippians 3:10).

"God is real!"

As we know Him and make known His passion, we restore the foundations of our faith, we walk in the power of His resurrection, and we become change agents of hope to a world in desperate need.

My prayerful desire and hope for you is that you will experience a fresh revelation of the work of the cross and the power of the resurrection.

one

BORN TO DIE

We all know the song, it might even be one of your favorite Christmas carols: "We three kings of orient are bearing gifts we've traversed afar ..."

Scripture does not specifically refer to kings but rather to "magi" or "wise men," and we are not given a headcount as to how many there were. Yet, we do know they did bear gifts, and we know what kind of gifts: gold, frankincense, and myrrh. All of these are burial items for a king.

And when they had come into the house, they saw the young Child with Mary His mother, and fell down and worshiped Him. And when they had opened their treasures, they presented gifts to Him: gold, frankincense, and myrrh (Matthew 2:11).

Do you understand the significance of this? Even at His birth, Jesus was recognized and honored as royalty! And from His very birth, Jesus was presented with items to prepare Him for His death.

In 2003, we saw the story of the crucifixion minister to thousands throughout the nation and around the world from a surprising source—Hollywood—with the release of *The Passion of the Christ*. With the movie's graphic depiction of the suffering Jesus endured for the joy set before Him—our salvations—came a new realization for many of the reality of the crucifixion. For others, the movie generated questions. As the cover of one national magazine boldly inquired, "Did Jesus really have to die?"

Even with the controversy surrounding the graphic violence involved in the scourging and death of Christ, an R rating would not be sufficient for an accurate portrayal of the extent He suffered, from the physical pain of the beatings to the emotional pain and loneliness of betrayal and false accusation. Crucifixion was a form of capitol punishment and considered the most humiliating and tormentful way to die. It is said that even the word "excruciating" did not exist until a word was needed to describe the pain of death by crucifixion.

The following account is a medical description of what Christ went through, written by the late Dr. C. Truman Thomas, whose widow, Jean, has graciously given us permission to print it once again:

> *The physical trauma of Christ begins with one of the initial aspects His suffering, the bloody sweat. It is interesting that the physician of the group, St. Luke, is the only one to mention this …*
>
> *Though very rare, the phenomenon of hematydrosis, or bloody sweat, is well documented. Under great emotional stress, tiny capillaries in the sweat glands can break, thus mixing blood with sweat. This process alone could have produced marked weakness, and possibly shock.*

After the arrest in the middle of the night, Jesus was brought before the Sanhedrin and Caiaphas, the high priest. A soldier struck Jesus across the face for remaining silent when questioned by Caiaphas. The palace guards then blindfolded Him and mockingly taunted Him to identify them as they passed, spat on Him, and struck Him in the face.

In the early morning, Jesus, battered and bruised, dehydrated and exhausted from a sleepless night, is taken across Jerusalem to the Praetorium of the fortress of Antonia. It was there, in response to the cries of the mob, that Pilate ordered Barnabas released and condemned Jesus to be scourged and crucified.

Preparations for the scourging are carried out. The prisoner is stripped of His clothing, and His hands tied to a post above His head. The Roman legionnaire steps forth with his flagrum (or flagellum) in his hand. This is a short whip consisting of several heavy leather thongs with two small balls of lead attached near the ends of each. The heavy whip is brought down with full force again and again across Jesus' shoulders, back, and legs. At first, the thongs cut through the skin only, then as the blows continue, they cut deeper into the subcutaneous tissues, producing first an oozing of blood from the capillaries and veins of the skin, and finally spurting arterial bleeding from vessels in the underlying muscles. The small balls of lead first produced deep bruises, which are broken open by the subsequent blows. Finally the skin of the back is hanging in long ribbons, and the entire area is an unrecognizable mass of torn, bleeding tissue.

*When it is determined by the centurion in charge
that the prisoner is near death, the beating is
finally stopped. The half-fainting Jesus is then
untied and allowed to slump to the stone
pavement, wet with His own blood. The Roman
soldiers see a great joke in the provincial Jew
claiming to be a king. They throw a robe across
his shoulders and place a stick in His hand for
a scepter. A small bundle of flexible branches
covered with long thorns is pressed into His scalp.
Again there is copious bleeding, the scalp being
one of the most vascular areas of the body.*

*After mocking Him and striking Him across the
face, the soldiers take the stick from His hand
and strike Him across the head, driving their
thorns deeper into His scalp. Finally they tire of
their sadistic sport, and the robe is torn from His
back. This had already become adherent to the
clots, to blood and serum in the wounds, and its
removal—just as in the careless removal of a
surgical bandage—causes excruciating pain,
almost as though He were again being whipped,
and the wounds again begin to bleed.*

*The heavy beam of the cross is then tied across
His shoulders, and the procession of the
condemned Christ, two thieves, and the execution
detail begins its slow journey. The weight of the
heavy wooden beam, together with the shock
produced by the copious blood loss, is too much.
He stumbles and falls. The rough wood of the
beam gauges into the lacerated skin and muscles
of the shoulders. He tries to rise, but human
muscles have been pushed beyond their
endurance.*

At Golgotha, the beam is placed on the ground,

and Jesus is quickly thrown backward with His shoulders against the wood. The legionnaire feels for the depression at the front of the wrist. He drives a heavy square wooden iron nail through the wrist, and deep into the wood. Quickly he moves to the other side, and repeats the action, being careful not to pull the arms too tightly, but to allow some flexing and movement. The beam is then lifted in place at the top of the stipes, and the titulus reading, 'Jesus of Nazareth, King of the Jews,' is nailed into place.

The left foot is pressed backward against the right foot, and with both feet extended and toes down, a nail is driven into the arch of each, as He pushes Himself upward to avoid the stretching torment. He places His full weight on the nail through His feet. Again, there is the searing agony of the nail tearing through the nerves between the metatarsal bones of the feet. As the arms fatigue, great waves of cramps sweep over the muscles, knotting them in deep, relentless, throbbing pain. With these cramps comes the inability to push Himself upward, hanging by His arms. The pectoral muscles are paralyzed, and the intercostal muscles are unable to act. Air can be drawn into the lungs but cannot be exhaled. Jesus fights to raise Himself in order to get even one short breath. Finally, carbon dioxide builds up in the lungs and in the bloodstream, and the cramps partially subside. Spasmodically, He is able to push Himself upward to exhale and bring in the life-giving oxygen.

Hours of this limitless pain, cycles of twisting, joint-rending cramps, intermittent partial asphyxiation, searing pain as tissue is torn from His lacerated back as He moves up and down against the rough timber. Then another agony begins, a deep crushing pain deep in the chest as the pericardium, slowly filling with serum, begins to compress the heart. The compressed heart is struggling to pump heavy, thick, sluggish blood into the tissues. The tortured lungs are making a frantic effort to grasp in small gulps of air. The markedly dehydrated tissues send their flood of stimuli to the brain.

Jesus gasps: "I thirst." He can feel the chill of death creeping through His tissues. With one last surge of strength, He once again presses His torn feet against the nail, straightens His legs, takes a deep breath, and utters His seventh and last cry, "Father, into Thy hands I commit My spirit."

Apparently, to make double sure of death, the legionnaire drives his lance through the fifth interspace between the ribs, upward through the pericardium, and into the heart. Immediately, there came out blood and water. We therefore have rather conclusive post-mortem evidence that our Lord died not the usual crucifixion (death by suffocation) but of heart failure (a broken heart) due to shock and constriction of the heart by fluid in the pericardium.

When we consider the joyous festivities that surround the Christmas holidays each year as we celebrate the birth of Jesus, it's hard to consider that the entire purpose of His birth was for Him to live a sinless life and be brutally crucified as the perfect sacrifice for our sins, fulfilling all the Old Testament Levitical sacrifices.

Before His death, Jesus commanded us to take communion in remembrance of Him: remembering what He has done, remembering that He was born to die so that we might have life. Each time we take communion, we are reminded of the high cost of love depicted on the cross of Calvary. He gave His life out of love, and through this display of love, our Prince of peace and our giver of hope gives us meaning, identity, and purpose.

"No greater love has this, than a man lay down His life for His friends" (John 15:13).

Why did He do this? Why did He leave His heavenly throne to come to earth, born to die? Hebrews 12:2-3 says it so beautifully and so clearly: He was willing to give Himself for us, to suffer shame and brutality and to endure the cross, for the joy set before Him.

What was the joy set before Him? *His joy was us!* To see you and me, God's very creation, reconciled to Himself, to be in relationship again with our Creator. Thus, He endured the cross, and now we have that same hope, we have that same joy as we fix our eyes on Jesus, the author and finisher of our faith, and we now partake in the joy He won for us on the cross, as we lead others to the truth of Calvary.

This is the joy that was set before Him, the reason He endured the cross, the reason He was born to die. In the midst of our own pain and trials, can we be the light that shines with that same joy—a joy unspeakable, a joy inexpressible—that others, too, might find their way home?

two

THE PERFECT SACRIFICE

Ever since the days of Adam and Eve, sin and temptation have produced a constant battleground in this world. What started as life in a beautiful garden was quickly turned into an existence characterized by sweat and tears. Peace was replaced by pain. Provision was replaced by poverty. Harmony was replaced by hatred.

Yet in the midst of the first human sin, there was also the first promise of redemption. God declared that even though the serpent would succeed in bruising mankind's heel, a human offspring would ultimately crush the serpent's head (Genesis 3:15). The curse of sin and death would be reversed. God's original intention would be fulfilled.

Through the work of the cross, we have hope and victory in Jesus the Christ. By faith in Christ we can be overcomers and find a victorious life in His name: *"And this is the victory that overcomes the world—our faith"* (1 John 5:4). This is a fulfillment of Jesus' promise that He came to give us life, and life more abundantly (John 10:10).

In 2004, I was invited to share and to participate in a "Juneteenth" ceremony, along with the Governor of Texas and other leaders, commemorating 139 years of freedom from slavery for African Americans in Texas. History shows that even though slavery was abolished in 1863, many slaves in the Gulf Coast region of Texas did not hear about it until the Emancipation Proclamation was read to them in 1865. For over two years, they were not aware of the good news that they were free.

Likewise, the message of the cross is good news, for we are liberated through the work of the cross! Yet many believers in Christ are not aware that they are free indeed. Like someone who is heir to a fortune but has never heard the news, many are living far short of God's intention.

Our Lord Jesus has won the victory for us, but the full benefits of this overwhelming triumph don't come to us automatically or inevitably. We have a role to play, too, for the benefits of His work on the cross must be appropriated by faith.

DESTROYING THE "DAM" OF A-DAM

The purpose of Christ's work on the cross was to reverse the disobedient work of Adam (see Romans 5). Just as Adam's work of *disobedience* occurred in a garden, Jesus chose *obedience* to the Father in another garden—the Garden of Gethsemane. Adam's curse was to toil by the sweat of his brow. But in Gethsemane's garden, Jesus sweat drops of blood to signify that the curse was about to be broken.

Nevertheless, obstacles can still hinder the flow of God's provision and life to us and through us. Picture a mighty river. Engineers are able to build a dam to stop its flow. In Romans 5, Paul teaches us that we were born with the nature of Adam (A dam!). This fallen nature is often called the Adamic nature or the sin nature. This is the very thing that blocks the free flow of God's love and life to our hearts. In order to reverse the effects of Adam's sin—destroy the "dam"—Jesus came to give His life (Romans 5:13-19). Jesus is our river of life, touching our lives and making us new creations in Him (2 Corinthians 5:17).

The sin nature is comprised of the body and soul, separated from the life-giving presence of the Spirit of God. The sin nature is radically different from the original image of God in which humans were created (Genesis 1:26, 1 Thessalonians 5:23). That is why Jesus said we must be "born again" (of the Spirit) if we want to see the kingdom of God (John 3:3-8). The work of the cross provides God's grace by which we can be regenerated—recreated into the original image of God.

When Adam and Eve sinned in the Garden of Eden, spiritual and physical death occurred. Sin produced death (Romans 6:23), which has been experienced by every man and woman since Adam. Until we come to the cross and surrender our lives to Jesus, we possess the nature of the first Adam. Not only is this sin nature susceptible to despair, defeat, disease, and sickness, but its ultimate fruit is hopelessness and death. The unregenerated heart is, by nature, a slave to all sorts of pride, lust, and temptation. However, the good news of the Gospel is this: We have been given a new heart and new nature in Jesus!

DELIVERANCE—ALL THE WAY BACK TO ADAM

One of the most tragic realities of today's church is that most believers are living far short of God's intention for them. We still bear the scars of the sin that came in the world through Adam, and often we have embraced a gospel that is impotent to change that situation to any great extent.

However, the true Gospel is more than instant forgiveness and "fire insurance." In addition to freeing us from *sin's penalty* (eternal judgment), the cross also offers to free us from *sin's power* over our lives. That's why Paul could boldly tell the Romans, *"Sin shall not have dominion over you, for you are not under law but under grace"* (Romans 6:14). There is a beautiful picture of this truth in Joshua 3, the story of Israel crossing the Jordan River to enter the Promised Land. Joshua was told to have the priests who bore the Ark of the Covenant step into the flooded river:

> *And it shall come to pass, as soon as the soles of the feet of the priests who bear the ark of the LORD, the Lord of all the earth, shall rest in the waters of the Jordan, that the waters of the Jordan shall be cut off, the waters that come down from upstream, and they shall stand as a heap* (Joshua 3:13).

The Jordan River was the only thing standing between the Israelites and their destiny. They could see the Promised Land, but the flooded river prevented them from entering it. Perhaps you find yourself in a similar place today. You have wandered for a while in the wilderness, and you finally are able to glimpse God's fantastic purpose for your life. But something is in the way—something that can only be overcome by an act of faith and obedience on your part.

When the priests stepped into the water, the flooding river was cut off. The waters from upstream stood in a heap, enabling the Israelites to cross over into their destiny. But look how far the waters backed up: *"... the waters which came down from upstream stood still, and rose in a heap very far away at **Adam**, the city that is beside Zaretan ..."* (Joshua 3:16a).

Do you see how wonderful this is? Not only did the waters part far enough to let the Israelites pass to the other side, but they backed up all the way to ADAM! In the same way, when Jesus died on the cross, the impact reverberated all the way back to Adam. While this might not be a textbook example of biblical exegesis, it is still a good analogy. Our great salvation offers both a *full pardon* and a *full empowerment* to overcome the effects of Adam's transgression. A life that is truly surrendered to Him is no longer without hope. We possess the life of Christ in our hearts, and that spiritual force offers to lead us through every situation in this earthly life. His life brings salvation, healing, and deliverance to all who are surrendered to Him—all the way back to the curse resulting from Adam's sin.

UNLOCKING THE BENEFITS OF COVENANT

How are such benefits of life, hope, and victory made available to us who are so undeserving? God uses a very special word to describe the basis of our relationship with Him. This word is *covenant!* Without a proper understanding of this great act of grace, we will not perceive the depth of God's love for us!

In the Bible, covenant is described as a deep and binding contractual relationship between two or more parties. Marriage is a good example of this kind of covenant. A marriage based on the Bible recognizes the same principles as a covenant: a lasting commitment, an exchange of vows and property, and the beginning of a new identity. The Bible also illustrates covenants made on the basis of protection (for example, Abraham and Lot) or friendship (Jonathan and David).

Regardless of the reason for entering into a covenant, however, there were certain basic procedures for what has been called "cutting the covenant." Let's look at some highly symbolic types and shadows that clearly speak of Jesus' perfect sacrifice for us.

When two parties decided to enter into covenant, they would take a lamb which was without spot or blemish and cut it down the middle (Genesis 15:1-18). The two parties would then make a circular walk between the two sections of the lamb, but in opposite directions. This would form a figure 8 (the infinity sign), which symbolized the eternal nature of the covenant being created. For those of you who are married, this is what your wedding rings symbolize—a never ending circle of covenant and love!

Next they would sprinkle the blood of the sacrificial lamb on a tree, particularly one that would outlive the parties to the covenant. This action symbolized that their covenant would bind not only them, but also their children and descendants.

Three more significant acts remained. They would exchange robes which were unique to the owners. Remember Joseph's coat of many colors in Genesis 37? This was unique to him. By exchanging robes, those making a covenant were signifying *mutual possession* of all their assets and liabilities. As the saying goes, "*Mi casa es su casa* (my house is your house)."

The same principle is true in our covenant with Jesus. All we had to offer Him was our robe of sin and unrighteousness, which God calls a filthy rag (Isaiah 64:6). In exchange, He graciously gave us His robe of righteousness. He gave us eternal life and the exceeding riches of His presence. Wow, what a deal!

Next, each party would exchange weapons of warfare— knives, swords, slings, bows and arrows, or whatever other armaments they were accustomed to using. This showed their commitment to *mutual defense*. To attack one of the covenant partners was the same as attacking both. That's why Paul can encourage the Romans, "*If God is for us, who can be against us?"* (Romans 8:31). In other words, God is our covenant partner! Anyone foolish enough to attack us is, in essence, attacking Him too. He clothes us with Himself so we can overcome the spiritual forces of wickedness. Finally, the covenant partners would sit down to share a covenant meal of bread and wine (for example, see Genesis 14:18). Again, the parallels are easy to see. The New Covenant is sealed by our partaking of communion—bread and wine to signify Jesus' body and blood. Peter explains that we have the amazing privilege to be *"partakers of the divine nature"* (2 Peter 1:4).

JESUS AND THE COVENANT

Jesus was the unspotted sacrificial lamb that was divided in two so we might enter into eternal covenant with the Father. It was His blood which was sprinkled on that "tree" (the cross) so we might live forever with Him. The bread and wine of the covenant meal is a beautiful picture of His body and blood, enabling us to enter into a relationship of communion with the Father.

After the tragedy of the twin towers on September 11, 2001, blood donors from around the nation responded in record numbers. Firefighters, police officers, and rescue workers perished attempting to rescue others. Yet even those heroic acts merely mirrored the greatest fireman of all, Jesus, who gave His life to rescue us from hell's flames! He was also the greatest blood donor who ever lived, shedding His blood so that we might live eternally!

His blood is the most precious substance in the entire universe. It is the indispensable key to the atonement of our sins. The Word of God proclaims that without the shedding of blood there is no remission of sins (Hebrews 9:22). And while we might tend to associate blood primarily with death, the Scriptures make it clear that *life* is in the blood (Leviticus 17:11, 17:14).

Shedding of blood is the very foundation of covenant-making in the Word of God, as well as in various cultures throughout the centuries. The central act in sealing a covenant was the shedding of blood, and the same is true for the New Covenant. Only through the blood of Jesus Christ can we have remission of sins and access into the very presence and throne of God.

In addition to shedding the blood of a sacrificial lamb, there was typically another kind of blood that was shed. Often the covenant partners would cut their hands or wrists, press the wounds together, and rub dirt or dye in the wound so that a permanent mark was left. In this way, the blood of both parties was mingled and they became, in effect, "blood brothers." The permanent marks on their bodies were perpetual signs of oneness and unity of heart, mind, and purpose. This was a lasting sign of covenant, which could be shown whenever needed. Although perfectly healed at His resurrection, Jesus carried upon Himself the permanent scars of His covenant with us. In response to Thomas' doubts, Jesus showed Him the marks of covenant (John 20:21-29), and these same marks will one day be seen by the whole world (Revelation 1:7).

IT'S ALL ABOUT HIM

The principles of covenant all point to Jesus. He is our covenant partner. He willingly became our sacrificial lamb on the cross so we could enter into a holy covenant with Him. The initiative was His, and to Him belongs all the glory.

But we who claim to be in covenant union with Him should take seriously our commitment to that covenant. When we enter into covenant with Jesus, we make a lifelong commitment to love and serve Him with all of our heart, soul, and might. We are called upon to offer ourselves as living sacrifices, holy and acceptable to God, which is our reasonable service (Romans 12:1).

When a consecrated heart is yielded to the Lord and committed to the covenant, obedience will flow naturally, like a waterfall down a mountain. What an awesome flow of divine life comes from such obedience! Deuteronomy 28:3-6 promises:

Blessed shall you be in the city, and blessed shall you be in the field. Blessed shall be the fruit of your body, the produce of your ground and the increase of your herds, the increase of your cattle and the offspring of your flocks. Blessed shall be your basket and your kneading bowl. Blessed shall you be when you come in, and blessed shall you be when you go out.

Not many of us today own cattle and sheep, but we have different things today God will bless just as much. I encourage you to get with God and meditate on the extravagant blessings He has planned for you—beyond anything you can dream or imagine (Ephesians 3:20).

Conversely, Deuteronomy 28:15-68 describes sobering warnings for those who willfully, actively, rebelliously disobey God. A heart that does not possess a covenant commitment will inevitably produce disobedience, forfeiting the benefits offered by covenant and the work of the cross. Hebrews 10:26-29 warns that if we sin willfully, there remains a fearful expectation of fiery judgment. Such willful sin is described as trampling the Son of God underfoot, counting the blood of the covenant as a common thing, and insulting the Spirit of grace.

After giving warnings reminiscent of Deuteronomy 28, the writer of Hebrews encourages his readers, saying, *"But, beloved, we are confident of better things concerning you, yes, things that accompany salvation, though we speak in this manner"* (Hebrews 6:9).

The apostle Paul, likewise, was utterly convinced that the One who began a good work in the Philippians would complete it until the day of Jesus Christ (Philippians 1:6). And look at his triumphant words of encouragement for the believers in Rome:

> *For whom He foreknew, He also predestined to be conformed to the image of His Son, that He might be the firstborn of many brethren ... What then, shall we say to these things? If God is for us, who can be against us? He who did not spare His own Son, but delivered Him up for us all, how shall He not with Him also freely give us all things? ... Who shall separate us from the love of Christ? Shall tribulation, or distress, or persecution, or famine, or nakedness, or peril, or sword? ... in all these things we are more than conquerors through Him who loved us. For I am persuaded that neither death nor life, nor angels nor principalities nor powers, nor things present nor things to come, nor height nor depth, nor any other created thing, shall be able to separate us from the love of God which is in Christ Jesus our Lord* (Romans 8:28-39).

Let's pause for a moment and thank our wonderful Savior for this awesome salvation won for us on the cross!

LEVITICAL OVERVIEW

Do you grasp how crucial it is to see Jesus as the perfect sacrifice? Have you come to appreciate the amazing freedom He won for us on the cross through His covenant blood? Without this firm foundation, it is impossible to move on to true maturity as a believer.

However, the work of the cross goes deeper still. The Gospel is more remarkable than we could ever imagine! Even those who boast of being "full Gospel" Christians have usually tasted only a fraction of what the Gospel is meant to provide. This has been described as someone who wades in a shallow stream and thinks he has experienced the depths of the ocean. As Paul encouraged the Ephesians, we serve a Lord who *"is able to do exceedingly abundantly above all that we ask or think, according to the power that works in us"* (Ephesians 3:20). It's time to go beyond superficial Christianity and receive the full benefits of the Gospel!

The complete ramifications of Jesus' passion begin to unfold when we look at the five basic sacrifices or offerings listed in the first seven chapters of Leviticus. Each one of these sacrifices points to Jesus and teaches us about a unique facet of His perfect sacrificial work.

Perhaps you have never realized *the entire Bible is about Jesus*—even the meticulous descriptions of sacrifices in the book of Leviticus. Jesus told the religious leaders of His day, *"You search the Scriptures, for in them you think you have eternal life; and these are they which testify of **Me**"* (John 5:39). The purpose of studying the Bible is more than just learning a set of religious facts! Its goal is to bring us into a vital relationship with our Lord Jesus. And that is our objective in examining the offerings described in Leviticus.

THE FIVE SACRIFICES JESUS FULFILLED

1. The first sacrifice described in Leviticus is the *burnt offering*, illustrating a total surrender to the Father's will. This is the essence of true worship: a heart that is in total submission to God.

> *And the priest shall burn all on the altar as a burnt sacrifice, an offering made by fire, a sweet aroma to the LORD* (Leviticus 1:9).

The burnt offering is a beautiful picture of Jesus' heart of love and consecration to His heavenly Father. It is listed first among the Levitical sacrifices because of its foundational role in pointing to the example of Christ. His passion was the ultimate fulfillment of the first and greatest commandment: to love the Lord our God with all our heart, with all our soul, and with all our might (Mark 12:28-34). His passionate prayer in the Garden of Gethsemane should be our cry as well: *"Not My will, but Yours, be done"* (Luke 22:42).

The burnt offering has profound implications for the meaning of discipleship. We try to make disciples by offering sermons, books, and classes, hoping that such resources will turn converts into fully devoted followers of Jesus. But, too often, we have left out the very first step in the discipleship process: dying to ourselves! Jesus could not have made this more clear: *"If anyone desires to come after Me, let him [first] deny himself, and take up his cross, and follow Me"* (Matthew 16:24). We often give the false impression that a person can follow Jesus without first denying himself and embracing the cross! Forgive us, Lord.

2. The second sacrifice was the *grain offering*, which was also referred to as the "meal offering." The grain offering represents the obedience of sinless service (grain without leaven), which naturally flows out of a surrendered life. It also represents communion with God. Through Jesus' sinless service, He became our grain offering so that we might freely commune with the Father.

The salt used in the grain offering points to Jesus as the salt of the earth, who came to cover and preserve us throughout eternity (Matthew 5:13). God wants us to be salty Christians! In a world filled with decay and death, we are to be preservatives. In a world that is often lifeless and bland, we are to supply flavor and fragrance. In a world where hearts are cold and hard, we are to be agents of softening, tenderizing, melting. But the impact of salt is diminished when it becomes compromised and adulterated. Restore us to purity, Lord!

3. The third sacrifice listed is the *peace offering*. The peace offering, also known as the fellowship offering, is a symbol of intimate friendship and reconciliation. It is a spontaneous offering which expresses one's gratitude and commitment to the Lord. Our fellowship with God and with one another, depicted in this offering, becomes like a sweet aroma.

There were three types of peace offerings: the praise, the vow, and the freewill. These are all a picture of Jesus' unbroken fellowship with the Father, which we, too, can experience through the work of the cross. Not only does Jesus *give* us peace, He *is* our peace! (See Ephesians 2:14.) He has broken down the wall of separation between us and God, between us and each other.

4. The fourth sacrifice was the *sin offering.* It was a mandatory offering that typified Jesus as the guilt substitute for our sins. He, and He alone, is our guilt-bearer. As our sin offering, Jesus paid a debt which He did not owe, because we owed a debt we could not pay. Once and for all, He took away our guilt and paid sin's penalty, which is death (Romans 6:23).

Many Christians have only scratched the surface in their understanding of who they are in Christ because of His sin offering. Yes, we are forgiven, but that is only the beginning. He has also given us a new nature which is free to serve Him and not our former lusts! Paul shares this amazing news with the Corinthians: *"For He [God] made Him [Jesus] who knew no sin to be sin for us, that we might become the righteousness of God in Him* (2 Corinthians 5:21). Did you catch that fantastic message? In Christ you have received not only forgiveness, but the very righteousness of God! If you truly see that, you will want to shout!

5. The fifth and final sacrifice was known as the *trespass offering,* or the guilt offering. This offering represents our need for Jesus to heal the damage done by sin. From Adam's sin (Genesis 3) to our own, acts of rebellion have always caused damage. But Jesus is our Savior, our Healer, and our Deliverer. He came to destroy the works of the devil (1 John 3:8) and to make all things new (Revelation 21:5). I John 1:9 promises, *"If we confess our sins, He is faithful and just to **forgive us** our sins and to **cleanse us** from **all** unrighteousness."* This is good news! As Isaiah 53:8

prophetically declared hundreds of years before Christ's passion: *"For the transgressions of My people He was stricken."*

An interesting aspect of the *trespass* offering is that God expected the transgressor to make restitution whenever possible:

> *And he shall make restitution for the harm that he has done in regard to the holy thing, and shall add one-fifth to it and give it to the priest. So the priest shall make atonement for him with the ram of the* trespass *offering, and it shall be forgiven him"* (Leviticus 5:16).

In light of Jesus' great grace in forgiving our sins, we may think this requirement for restitution is somewhat out of place. Isn't Jesus' blood the sole hope for our forgiveness? Indeed it is, but there is also an aspect of accountability for those who would bring a trespass offering. If we expect to be right with God, we must do whatever we can to make things right with any person we have wronged (Matthew 5:23-24). When we ask the Lord to forgive our trespasses, we should be sure that we have also forgiven those who have trespassed against us (Matthew 6:12, Matthew 6:14-15, Mark 11:35-36, Matthew 18:21-35).

HOW SHOULD WE RESPOND?

Consider this: In one moment of time 2,000 years ago, Jesus fulfilled each of these sacrifices for us. He was the perfect sacrifice, setting us free from Satan's grip and bringing us into the presence of the Father. No longer do we need to sacrifice animals, for their blood under the Old Testament was just a foreshadow of the blood of Jesus, which was shed once and for all to reconcile us to God (Hebrews 10:1-23).

How should we respond to such a great sacrifice? To such amazing love? After a clear presentation of God's unmerited favor toward us in Christ, the apostle Paul goes on to tell the Romans how we should respond: *"I beseech you therefore, brethren, by the mercies of God, that you present your bodies a living sacrifice, holy, acceptable to God, which is your reasonable service"* (Romans 12:1).

Because of His grand sacrifice for us, it is only reasonable for us, in turn, to offer ourselves as living sacrifices to Him. Accurately seeing the passion *of* Christ will inevitably lead to passion *for* Christ.

four

TOTAL SURRENDER TO THE FATHER'S WILL:

SURRENDER, CLEANSING AND FIRE
THE BURNT OFFERING PART I

Has there come a time in your life when the revelation of Jesus and His work on the cross became so real that you desired to yield yourself fully to His will? Perhaps you once recited the Lord's Prayer with shallow platitudes and religious incantations, then the words began to take life within you. Your fleshly creed of "*my* kingdom come, *my* will be done" was replaced by the new cry, "*Your* kingdom come, *Your* will be done." Even the act of water baptism took on a new meaning, outwardly demonstrating your heart's desire to totally die to your sinful nature and walk in righteousness as a new person in Christ Jesus.

Again, this reality of the New Covenant was foreshadowed in the Old Testament. A prominent part of the tabernacle or temple was the Brazen Altar, or altar of burnt sacrifice. This altar was set in the outer section of the tabernacle or temple, and it was the first thing to confront a worshipper upon entering the courtyard. On this altar, the burnt offering was offered up to God. This became symbolic of a place of total submission and surrender.

This is a beautiful picture of Jesus' total surrender to the will of the Father. He became our burnt offering on the cross so that we might become His *living* sacrifice (Romans 12:1-2). To have an obedient heart, in total submission to God's will, is the highest form of worship.

ABSOLUTE SURRENDER, ABSOLUTE DELIGHT

When the burnt offering is described in Leviticus, there is an intriguing use of the word "all" regarding the sacrificed animal:

> *...And the priest shall burn **all** on the altar as a burnt sacrifice, an offering made by fire, a sweet aroma to the LORD* (Leviticus 1:9b).

> *...Then the priest shall bring it **all** and burn it on the altar; it is a burnt sacrifice, an offering made by fire, a sweet aroma to the LORD* (Leviticus 1:13b).

A unique feature of this offering was its radical nature: when making a sacrifice from the herd, ALL of the animal was consumed by the fire of God. Absolutely nothing was exempt. The message was clear: We must give *all* of our heart and soul and mind and strength as a living sacrifice to Him (Deuteronomy 6:4-9, Mark 12:28-34). The lordship of Jesus means nothing remains in us that is not consumed by His holy fire. Nothing remains that is not subject to His authority. It all belongs to Him, for He purchased it all on the cross.

It is crucial to understand the burnt offering if we are to build a firm foundation regarding the other pearls God has hidden for us in His Word. Leviticus 1:3 says, *"If his offering is a burnt sacrifice of the herd, let him offer a male without blemish; he shall offer it of his own free will at the door of the tabernacle of meeting before the Lord."*

The "male without blemish" phrase speaks of two primary things: First and foremost, it teaches that the Messiah, Jesus, would be a male "without blemish," or without sin. He lived a perfect life, which was a necessary requisite for becoming the perfect sacrifice for our sins (Hebrews 2:17-18, Hebrews 4:14-15).

Many people today—even many professing Christians— fail to see the importance of Jesus' sinlessness. "He was just a good man ... an insightful teacher...or perhaps even a prophet," they say. But such statements fall far short of what the Bible teaches about our glorious Lord Jesus. The truth of His sinless life is testified to throughout the New Testament, but was already foreshadowed in the burnt offerings described in Leviticus. As the sacrificial lambs were examined to see if they were flawed in any way, so was Jesus examined by His accusers. The result was Pilate's threefold declaration: *"I find no fault in Him at all"* (John 18:38, John 19:4, John 19:6).

Second, the "without blemish" phrase speaks to you and me. God wants our lives, through Jesus, to be without spot or blemish. He desires that we come before Him without false or impure motives, totally open and without guile. Peter tells us, *"...but as He who called you is holy, you also be holy in all your conduct, because it is written, 'Be holy, for I am holy'"* (1 Peter 1:15-16, quoting Leviticus 11:44-45).

Verse 3 goes on to say that a person giving a burnt offering should do so *"of his own free will."* Instead of just being an act of duty or compulsion, this offering is meant to spring from our free will—our heart of love and devotion to the Lord. Throughout history, and even in some animistic religions today, people have often offered sacrifices to their gods out of fear—as acts of appeasement. However, the Levitical offerings were fundamentally different. Stemming from *free will*, these offerings were acts of *worship*. When we come before God with a willing heart, we are engaging in one of the highest forms of worship. Instead of being robots forced to worship our Creator, we have been given the privilege to passionately worship Him out of our own free will. Consider this: *God is not looking for clones of modern-day Christianity, but for worshippers and imitators of Christ.* Religious duty would make us clones, but true worship transforms us into the image of Christ. Even as Jesus yielded His will in total submission to the Father, so should we. This is more than duty; it is delight.

THE CHOICE

Leviticus 1:4 paints an intriguing picture of the choice Jesus had to face at the end of His ministry: *"Then he shall put his hand on the head of the burnt offering, and it will be accepted on his behalf to make atonement for him."* The *Wycliffe Bible Commentary* states that the Hebrew text for "put his hand on the head" signifies "pressing with vigor upon the animal's head." We do not know all the details of the sacrificial ritual, but the intent here was apparently to show a passionate transfer of sin. This was not a passive endeavor but clearly involved a tremendous expenditure of physical and mental energy.

When we look at Jesus on the cross, we see this same passion and energy. From His sacrificial life, to His struggle in the garden, to His obedience unto death—there was complete dedication and commitment to becoming a perfect sacrifice, in total submission to the Father's will. Upon Jesus, the spotless Lamb of God, there was a "pressing with vigor" of all eternity's sin and rejection. In one pivotal moment of time, God *"made Him who knew no sin [Jesus] to be sin for us, that we might become the righteousness of God in Him"* (2 Corinthians 5:21). Jesus became the fulfillment of the Levitical burnt sacrifices, exemplifying total surrender and obedience to the Father.

Of course, the lambs sacrificed under the Old Covenant had no choice in the matter. There was no way for them to protest, "Sorry guys, but I really don't want to go through with this!" Jesus, on the other hand, made a conscious choice. He could have called 12 legions of angels to rescue Him, but He didn't (Matthew 26:53). Jesus made it clear that no one was able to take His life from Him. Rather, He laid His life down *voluntarily* (John 10:17-18).

But there was a tremendous price associated with Jesus' choice. Leviticus 1:5 shows the huge cost of Jesus' choice— and, consequently, the choices we are called to make in His Name: *"He shall kill the bull before the Lord; and the priests, Aaron's sons, shall bring the blood and sprinkle the blood all around on the altar that is by the door of the tabernacle of meeting."*

The price? The blood of Jesus. The choice Jesus made required that blood be shed for sin, accompanied by all the agony and pain that came with it. Our stand for Christ may be painful and costly at times, but the end of the matter will always lead to resurrection and victory!

HAVE YOU BEEN 'SKINNED'?

The agony of Jesus' sacrifice is reflected in Leviticus 1:6, where it says that the burnt offering had to be skinned: *"And he shall skin the burnt offering and cut it into its pieces."* What does the word "skin" mean? In the King James Version, this same word is translated "flay." *Webster's Dictionary* provides three definitions for the word flay:

1. *To tear or strip away the skin or the outer covering.* If you have seen *The Passion of the Christ*, you realize the

extent to which Jesus' skin was stripped away by the Roman flogging. According to some traditions of church history, the apostle Thomas may have been martyred this way in India. This is the same use of the Hebrew word as we find it in Micah 3:3.

2. *To strip of possessions or to fleece.* Jesus was stripped of all His possessions and hung naked on a cross so that we might become rich in Him (2 Corinthians 8:9).

3. *To criticize harshly or to scold.* Hundreds of years prior to His death, it was prophesied about Jesus that He would be *"despised and rejected by men"* (Isaiah 53:3). The crowd, the soldiers, the thief on the cross all criticized Jesus with mocking, ridicule, and disdain.

In these three definitions we see the agony and pain Jesus endured on the cross as a result of His choice to lay down His life for us. Like the Old Testament burnt offerings, He was skinned (flayed) as a sacrifice for us. The scourgings which He endured literally took the skin off His back. He was criticized, reproved, ridiculed and scolded on our behalf. On the cross He lay totally exposed before the Lord and naked before the world, taking our sins upon Himself.

What does all this mean to us? It means that, through Jesus, we can come to a place of total submission to the Father's will. When we make this choice, we must realize that at times the Lord will "flay" our flesh in order to expose every part of our lives before Him. He will skin us of guile and false motivations as we cry out to Him, "Lord, I surrender every part of my life to You. I lie before You open and exposed. You have the right to be Lord of every part of my life."

Two things come to mind when we read Leviticus 1:9: *"...but he shall wash its entrails and its legs with water. And the priest shall burn ALL on the altar as a burnt sacrifice, an offering made by fire, a sweet aroma to the Lord."*

Washing the "entrails and legs" speaks of the cleansing of sin from our innermost being when we choose to open ourselves up to the Lord and the sanctifying power of His Spirit. After David's sin with Bathsheba was exposed, He cried out to the Lord for this inner cleansing:

> *Wash me thoroughly from my iniquity, and cleanse me from my sin...Behold you desire truth in the inward parts, and in the hidden part You make me to know wisdom. Purge me with hyssop, and I shall be clean; wash me, and I shall be whiter than snow...Create in me a clean heart...* (Psalm 51:2, 6-7, 10).

Many people are concerned only with cleaning up their outward reputations, but David wanted something more. He wanted a cleansing that would bring God's truth all the way to his "inward parts" and "hidden part"—the part of his heart only the Lord would see. While people often are content that their righteousness is merely "whiter than their *neighbor's*," David wanted a new heart that was "whiter than *snow*" (an objective standard).

The use of the word "ALL" is significant here, because it conveys the notion that ALL is given to the lordship of Jesus Christ. Before all can be given to Him, all must be exposed. Every part of our innermost being is laid open before Him, that He might work His wondrous works in us. When this is done, we literally become a burnt sacrifice, an offering made by fire, a sweet fragrance to the Lord. When an offering is consumed by the fire of God in the Bible, it means the offering has been accepted by God.

With God's acceptance comes His anointing and presence. It is His desire that we would present our bodies *"a living sacrifice, holy, acceptable to God, which is [our] reasonable service"* (Romans 12:1). He wants to consume us with His very presence, that we might be empowered to demonstrate His life.

ALL THAT WE HAVE—BUT NOT WHAT WE DON'T HAVE

Leviticus 1:14 introduces a new theme regarding burnt offerings: *"And if the burnt sacrifice of his offering to the Lord is of birds, then he shall bring his offering of turtledoves or young pigeons."* Note that different types of animals are allowed for use in these sacrifices: bullocks, sheep, goats, and now turtledoves and pigeons. The reason different types of animals are specified for sacrifice is that people had different economic situations. Some were not wealthy enough to own bullocks, sheep, or goats.

Remember the story of the "widow's mite" in Luke 21:1-4? The widow didn't have much, but she offered what she had. Jesus commented that she gave ALL she had. Consequently, her offering was counted acceptable, more valuable than all the riches being offered by those who were wealthy.

This is the kind of situation God is making provision for in Leviticus 1:14. He is giving people the opportunity to simply bring what they can afford. If they could not bring a bullock to the Brazen Altar, they were welcome to present their hearts before Him with something as simple as a pigeon! The real issue here is our willingness to give our ALL to the Lord. The issue has nothing to do with comparing our sacrifice to someone else's. The sole question is whether we have given our ALL.

The issue is not our bank account but our heart. May we be able to say, "Lord, You have the right to every part of my life. I trust You with my life, finances, relationships, career—with everything. Lord, may my heart—my innermost being—always be open before You."

PERFECT FULFILLMENT BY JESUS

Jesus, our perfect sacrifice, literally fulfilled every one of the points we have discussed so far, and much more. Every facet of the ritual of the burnt offering directs us to Jesus. Hundreds of years before Jesus walked the earth, the pages of the Old Testament testified about His glorious work on the cross.

Psalm 22 gives us a compelling picture of what Jesus endured on the cross, and it sheds further light on how some facets of the Levitical offerings were fulfilled by Him. Psalm 22 begins: *"My God, my God, why have You forsaken Me?"* Yes, these are the very words of Jesus during His last living moments on the cross! (Matthew 27:46)

Do you remember when Jesus was beaten by the chief priests and elders? Matthew 26:67 says, *"Then they spat on His face and beat Him; and others struck Him with the palms of their hands."* The religious leaders, as representatives of the people, spit on Jesus and struck Him with the palms of their hands. In so doing, they illustrated the impartation of sin that Leviticus 1:4 described hundreds of years before. In effect, they were unwittingly fulfilling that Scripture, where the sinner laid his hands upon the sacrificial lamb in order to transfer his sin to the animal substitute. These leaders may have been the "strong bulls of Bashan" referenced prophetically in Psalm 22:12-13. The net result was to carry out God's ultimate plan, as described in Isaiah 53:6b: *"...And the LORD has laid on Him the iniquity of us all."*

NOT A BONE BROKEN

Exodus 12:46, Numbers 9:12, and Leviticus 1:17 all teach that the bones of the sacrificial animals were not to be broken as they were being sacrificed before the Lord. This is in contrast to the usual details of a crucifixion, for the person crucified often had his legs broken to speed his death, as he was no longer able to lift his torso to exhale and inhale, thus hastening his suffocation. However, this was not done in Jesus' case—so that the Scriptures could be fulfilled—because Jesus had already died (John 19:31-36). Instead, the soldiers pierced his side, releasing a flow of blood and water. This was also a fulfillment of Old Testament Scripture, Psalm 22:14-15, which states prophetically about Jesus' crucifixion:

> *"I am poured out like water, and all My bones are out of joint; My heart is like wax; it has melted within Me. My strength is dried up like a potsherd, and My tongue clings to My jaws; You have brought Me to the dust of death."*

When this passage says that Jesus would be "poured out like water," it means that His body would dehydrate through the ordeal of the cross. Muscles and tendons are what hold our bones and joints in place. They are comprised of more than 70% water. When severe dehydration occurs, muscles and tendons break down, lose their elasticity, and are unable to properly support the skeletal structure. In other words, hanging on a cross would basically cause certain joints (especially the shoulders) to come out of socket.

This, of course, is why Psalm 22:14 prophetically points to Jesus when saying, *"My bones are out of joint."* In effect, they were being divided or "split" (as Leviticus 1:17 teaches) through the dehydration process.

MORNING, EVENING, AND *ALWAYS!*

While burnt offerings from the people were voluntary, in Exodus 29:36-46 God commands the priests of Israel to sacrifice two offerings daily on behalf of the people. These were to be burnt offerings, one in the morning and one in the evening. The morning sacrifice was presented on the third hour of the day (9 a.m.) and the evening sacrifice on the ninth hour of the day (3 p.m.).

The parallel? Jesus was hung on the cross on the third hour of the day (Mark 15:24-25), at the exact time as the priests were sacrificing the morning burnt offering in anticipation of Israel's coming Messiah. Likewise, Jesus breathed His last breath on the ninth hour (Matthew 27:45-51). This was exactly the same time the priests were making their second burnt offering of the day, in prophetic type of His sacrifice for our sins. Yes, Jesus fulfilled every jot and tittle of the Law, and He also wants to fulfill every need and desire we have to honor and glorify Him.

What a wonderful Savior! Of His own free will, He died for us that we might have life. He was flayed for us, ripped apart for us, and offered in total surrender for us. He was ridiculed, mocked, scorned, and reproached by those He died for. He was our example through it all. Even at the moment of final testing, He prayed to the Father, *"...not My will, but Yours, be done"* (Luke 22:42).

So what does so great an example mean for us, the sheep of His pasture? For one thing, we need to understand that Jesus' passion *for* us was meant to produce a passion *in* us. This is not meant to be an experience of momentary goose bumps, but rather a continual reality. Look at this amazing principle regarding the burnt offering:

> *And the fire on the altar shall be kept burning on it; it shall not be put out. And the priest shall burn wood on it every morning, and lay the burnt offering in order on it; and he shall burn on it the fat of the peace offerings. A fire shall always be burning on the altar;* ***it shall never go out*** (Leviticus 6:12-13).

Wow! God wants to light a fire in us that "shall never go

out"! Yes, there were burnt offerings at two specific times of day, but the fire on the altar was not to be limited by that. The fire was to burn continuously. Too often, Christians live their spiritual lives on the basis of specific events, such as Sunday church services or other gatherings. While such events are wonderful, they are meant to just be part of a continual life of worship—a fire in our hearts that will never go out.

Are you ready to pray with me for a new breakthrough of God's presence and power in our lives? Are you willing to be "flayed" in order to be laid wide open before the Father, saying, "Lord, You have the right to expose every element of my life before You. Not my will, but Your will be done"?

Are you ready to experience God's fire? If so, join me in this passionate prayer:

> *"Consume me with Your fire, and never let the fire of Your presence go out in my life. I de*sire my daily walk with You *to be an act of continual worship. Oh, Lord, give me a clean heart, a right spirit, and a renewed mind. Show me, lead me, and teach me Your ways."*

If we are to make a substantial difference in this world, we must be consumed with the continual fire of God's presence. May the glory of our Lord Jesus be manifested more powerfully than ever before through His bride, His church!

five

OBEDIENCE TO THE FATHER'S WILL

WASH AND BE FRAGRANT!
THE BURNT OFFERING PART II

As critical as it is to surrender ourselves fully to the Lord as living sacrifices, our journey does not end there, which we see as we take a momentary detour from our study of Leviticus to examine instructions God gave to the priests in the book of Exodus. After the altar of burnt sacrifice, the priest walked up to the next object in the tabernacle or temple: a water basin called the laver.

> *He made the laver of bronze and its base of bronze, from the bronze mirrors of the serving women who assembled at the door of the tabernacle of meeting* (Exodus 38:8).

> *And you shall set the laver between the tabernacle of meeting and the altar, and put water in it* (Exodus 40:7).

At this laver of water, the priest washed his hands and feet, symbolizing the washing away of our sins. The laver also typifies water baptism. This is a fitting progression, for after we totally surrender our lives to the Lord (similar to a burnt offering), we follow Him in water baptism (the laver). As Scripture teaches us, *"Old things have passed away; behold, all things have become new"* (2 Corinthians 5:17). When we totally surrender our lives to the Lord, we are ready for water baptism—a public statement of what the Lord has done in our hearts and lives. Even as the priest did in the Old Testament on our behalf, we as kings and priests under the New Covenant physically demonstrate the cleansing of our hearts by this act of obedience to the Lord. In water baptism we are saying, "My life is different in Christ. I am not the same person I was before I came into relationship with Him."

ENTERING THE INNER COURT

From the laver (water basin), the priest entered into the inner court of the tabernacle or temple. Remember, only a priest from the tribe of Levi could go any further into the tabernacle or temple. The Levitical priest took these steps on our behalf, however, and his work was perfectly fulfilled by Jesus, our High Priest. By His own blood, He entered the heavenly temple on our behalf. He made a way for us to enter the holy place through His blood.

The porch or entrance to the temple building faced east, directly opposite the East Gate, which was the entrance to the temple grounds proper. Against the left side of the south wall of the inner court, the Lord set the great golden lampstand. The light from these lamps illuminated the entire inner court, even as the Holy Spirit comes to illuminate the truth in the "inner court" of the temple of our hearts!

Against the right side of the inner court God placed the table of showbread, which held the bread of covenant. As a type of Jesus' body which was broken and sacrificed for us, the table of showbread speaks of the sweet communion with Him that is available because of what He did for us on the cross.

The entire Old Testament is full of beautiful types, shadows, and pictures pointing to the tremendous cost of Jesus' love for us on Calvary. The pages of the Old Testament wonderfully illustrate such New Testament truths as total surrender, water baptism, illumination of the Holy Spirit, the breaking of bread, and communion with God! Through the placement of these items in the temple, God is saying, "I want you to come to Me with a right heart. I want you to allow the Holy Spirit to illuminate My truth in your life, in your body, which is now My temple."

THE HOLY OF HOLIES

Directly opposite the entrance to the inner court (30 feet away) hung a massive veil, which "veiled" Israel from the consuming fire of God's presence. Only once a year, on the Day of Atonement, was the high priest permitted to pass through the veil and offer the blood of the sacrifice on the Mercy Seat. Hebrews 10:20 teaches us this veil represented the body of Jesus, which veiled the glory of God in His life while He walked the earth.

Praise God, this veil was miraculously torn open when Jesus died on the cross, enabling us now to have bold access to the very presence of God! From top to bottom, this massive veil was ripped in two, exposing the Most Holy Place or Holy of Holies. As Jesus' flesh was being ripped on our behalf, the temple veil was ripped to open our way to the heart of God. This dramatic supernatural act gave us immediate access to God's inner sanctum, the place of full intimacy with Him (see Matthew 27:51, Hebrews 10:10-22, and Hebrews 4:16).

The Ark of the Covenant resided in the Holy of Holies,

representing God's manifested presence. In the days of
Israel's journeys in the wilderness, this Ark was carried with
them, following a cloud of glory by day and fire by night.

THE ALTAR OF INCENSE

Encountering the living God in the Holy of Holies
becomes the end of the road for all who choose to place
their full hope in Jesus, following Him into the Father's
presence. However, we must not forget the piece of temple
furniture that was just outside the veil: the Altar of Incense.
Upon this altar burned spices that released a sweet-smelling
aroma. The incense rising up to God before the veil
represented the prayers of Jesus on our behalf, as well as
our prayers in His Name.

Remarkably, this Old Testament picture foreshadows a
heavenly, end-time reality:

> *Now when He had taken the scroll, the four living
> creatures and twenty-four elders fell down before
> the Lamb, each having a harp, and golden bowls
> of incense, which are the prayers of the saints*
> (Revelation 5:8).

How we need these prayers today—prayers that will
release the sweet aroma of incense, both in heaven and on
earth! Believers who regularly worship at the Altar of Incense
are destined to have a powerful role in spreading this great
fragrance throughout the earth, as Paul tells the Corinthians:

> *Now thanks be to God who always leads us in
> triumph in Christ, and through us diffuses the
> fragrance of His knowledge in every place. For
> we are to God the fragrance of Christ among those
> who are being saved and among those who are
> perishing. To the one we are the aroma of death
> leading to death, and to the other the aroma of*

life leading to life. And who is sufficient for these things? (2 Corinthians 2:14-16)

CONNECTING THE DOTS

Sadly, many believers still see the Scriptures as a series of random and unconnected dots. The two Testaments seem to have nothing to do with each other, and it is difficult to see the common threads that run through the early chapters of the Bible all the way to its concluding chapters.

It's time to connect the dots! When we do so, the seemingly random events and chapters form a beautiful tapestry, a stunningly accurate picture of our glorious Lord Jesus.

So what dots can we already connect based on our journey through Leviticus? We first saw the love of Jesus, the heart of total surrender to the Father's will as illustrated by the burnt offerings at the Brazen Altar. I believe the burnt offering is listed first because total surrender and obedience to God are the highest forms of love and worship to Him—the very fulfillment of His holy laws and commandments (Deuteronomy 6:4-9, Matthew 22:36-40). This heart attitude is the very foundation of our journey to the manifested presence of God. We then see the washing of our sins through baptism and new resurrected life in Christ at the brazen altar.

As we cultivate a relationship of peace and communion with Him by the total surrender of our lives, we are ready to come to the Altar of Incense—that spiritual place of prayer and intercession fueled by a genuine heart after God. Prayers at the Altar of Incense are not directed by our intellect or lip service, but by an unquenchable passion for the Father's heart.

When we come boldly into His presence in this way, beyond the torn veil, crying "Abba Father," then Jesus' promise will truly come to pass in our lives:

And whatever you ask in My name, that I will do, that the Father may be glorified in the Son. If you ask anything in My name, I will do it (John 14:13-14).

When we delight in Him, He will grant us the desires of our hearts (Psalm 37:4). We need not come timidly or tentatively. He beckons us to come boldly.

JESUS' SINLESS SERVICE

THE GRAIN OFFERING PART 1

The **grain offering**, also known as the meal or meat offering, depicts Christ's sinless service. "Meat," the word used in the King James Version, is an old English word for "food" or "grain." In this case, the offering generally involved very fine flour. The grain offering described in Leviticus 2 points to Jesus as our Bread of Life and the one who offered sinless service to the Father.

As with the other offerings, the grain offering depicts both Jesus' work on the cross and the way we should live through Him. The grain offering pictures Jesus as the Perfect Man, totally without sin, living in joyous obedience to the will of the Father on behalf of sinful man (Hebrews12:2). It also symbolizes joy and thanksgiving to God for His salvation, redemption, and reconciliation, as well as joyous gratitude for His provisions. There is much to rejoice about, because the work of the cross enables us to have true communion with God and others.

In Leviticus 2:1-4, several key words provide life-changing insight about the grain offering:

> *When anyone offers a grain offering to the LORD, his offering shall be of fine flour. And he shall pour oil on it, and put frankincense on it. He shall bring it to Aaron's sons, the priests, one of whom shall take from it his handful of fine flour and oil with all the frankincense. And the priest shall burn it as a memorial on the altar, an offering made by fire, a sweet aroma to the LORD. The rest of the grain offering shall be Aaron's and his sons'. It is a most holy offering of the offerings to the LORD made by fire. And if you bring as an offering a grain offering baked in the oven, it shall be unleavened cakes of fine flour mixed with oil, or unleavened wafers anointed with oil.*

Verse 1 makes reference to "fine flour." Flour is made from seed kernels of a grain such as wheat, barley, or rye. Through a tedious, labor-intensive process, these kernels are ground into a powder. Fine flour is made by sifting the ground kernels and then grinding and sifting them again. The result is a very fine powder which is "perfect" in its uniformity and consistency.

The grain kernels can be ground by hand with a wheel or by using an ox or bullock with a millstone around its neck. The ox is a biblical type of suffering servanthood. The ox also represents one of the four prophetic portraits of the Messiah-King who would conquer sin by His sinless service and by serving others (Ezekiel 1:10, Revelation 4:7, John 13:1-17).

THE SEED, THE OIL, AND THE FRANKINCENSE

"Seed" in the Bible is symbolic of the Word of God and those who are "sons of the kingdom" (Matthew 13:3-43).

Jesus is our Living Word and the Word that became flesh (John 1:1-4). He was crushed, beaten, and bruised for our iniquities (Isaiah 53:4-5, Mark 14:65). He was crushed, beaten, and bruised, during both His life of service and during His passion on the cross. He Himself was the original SEED, the grain of wheat that fell into the ground and died so that it would ultimately reap a great harvest (John 12:23-26). Jesus was sifted for our sakes (Matthew 4:1-11, Matthew 26:36-46), and no impurities were found in Him. Every motive, thought, word, and deed was found perfect in the sight of God. In this way, "fine flour" becomes a biblical type for the perfection of our Lord, Jesus Christ. Only that kind of perfection could produce the fruit of unspoiled obedience before the Father. By the power of His seed in us, we are able to overcome the deeds of the flesh (1 John 3:9).

Leviticus 2:1 also mentions "oil" and "frankincense." Oil in Scripture is symbolic of the anointing of the Holy Spirit. When the priest took the "fine flour" (the perfection of Christ) and fashioned it into a "body" of bread, he then anointed it with oil. We see a symbolic representation of the divine nature being formed into a body of flesh and then being anointed and empowered to fulfill a particular purpose (John 1:1-34). The purpose illustrated in the grain offering was that Jesus would live a perfect life of obedience. We are not only justified by His life, He also baptizes us and anoints us with His very presence so we might manifest that life as well. The Scriptures teach that Jesus had the Spirit without measure (John 3:34), and He earnestly wants to baptize us with that same Spirit for His glory.

Frankincense is a fragrant spice that was often used in preparation for burial. Jesus, our grain offering, was born to die. When the magi from the East came to honor Jesus as a young child, they brought gifts of gold, frankincense, and myrrh (Matthew 2:1-11). And just prior to the betrayal and crucifixion, Mary anointed His head with an alabaster flask filled with a fragrant and very costly spikenard oil (Mark 14:3-9). Jesus, speaking of Mary's act of faith and love, said that it would be spoken of as a perpetual memorial: *"She has done what she could. She has come beforehand to anoint My body for burial"* (Mark 14:8b).

There is a stunning parallel between Mary's act and the Levitical grain offering, which also brought about a memorial and a sweet-smelling aroma: *"...And the priest shall burn it as a memorial on the altar, an offering made by fire, a sweet aroma to the LORD"* (Leviticus 2:2). Mary's act of worship fulfilled this prophetic memorial by anointing Jesus in preparation for His work on the cross! The accomplishment of God's purpose in His Son was a "sweet aroma" to the LORD.

When the priest burned the fine flour, oil, and frankincense as a memorial before the Lord, a wonderful fragrance filled the air. The sweetness of the offering pleased God in the same way a sweet-smelling fragrance pleases our physical senses. This part of the grain offering teaches us of His joy in our acts of love and worship.

BREAD AND MANNA

The grain offering also depicts Jesus as our Bread of Life and our Manna. In Leviticus 2:4-5 we see the word "unleavened" used with the grain offering. Leaven is symbolic of two different things in Scripture. Depending on the context, leaven can represent the powerful, expanding kingdom of heaven (Matthew 13:33) or it can be symbolic of arrogance and sin, which also spreads and expands (1 Corinthian 5:5-7).

Since leaven is forbidden in the grain offering, we can see that the context is speaking of leaven as representative of sin and rebellion. Bread made from unleavened flour is simply teaching life without sin. Jesus was "unleavened" as He lived a sinless life. He was a sinless servant who was fully tempted but fully pure.

Through Jesus' sanctifying presence in our hearts, God wants to remove the corrupting power of "leaven" from our lives. As Jesus did, we need to go before the Lord without pretense. Anything that causes us to be puffed up with pride is a source of leaven in our offering. Of course, we ourselves are not sinless, but Jesus in us is. Jesus said of Himself:

*Most assuredly, I say to you, Moses did not give you the bread from heaven, but My Father gives you **the true bread from heaven.** For the bread of God is He who comes down from heaven and gives life to the world* (John 6:32-33).

I am the bread of life. *He who comes to Me shall never hunger, and he who believes in Me shall never thirst* (John 6:35).

*…Jesus took bread, blessed it and broke it, and gave it to them and said, "Take, eat: this is **My body"*** (Mark 14:22).

He is the bread we need! Let us commune with Him and receive every spiritual nutrient we need for life and godliness (2 Peter 1:2-4).

THE REFINING FIRE

Leviticus 2:9 says: *"Then the priest shall take from the grain offering a memorial portion, and burn it on the altar. It is an **offering made by fire,** a sweet aroma to the LORD."* The word "fire" is figurative of God's refining fire. When we are "tried" by God's fire, everything that is not of Him is burned off in the flames (1 Corinthians 3:10-15). Jesus, our grain offering, was tried by the fire of God's judgment against sin and was found totally sinless. He overcame sin and death, and His indwelling presence offers to make us victorious as well (John 16:33, 1 John 4:4, 1 John 5:4).

After the portion of the grain offering was burnt on the altar, the rest was given to Aaron and his sons for their use. This was one way God provided for the needs of those in His priestly service. As long as the priests were faithful in their ministry—teaching God's Word and leading people in paths of righteousness—they were provided for. However, when the priests treated sin lightly (for example, see the book of Malachi), people fell away from God and no longer brought their offerings.

What happens when people fail to bring their offerings? The priests are forced to find other ways to provide for themselves, and their God-ordained ministry is neglected.

Compare the priests' daily eating of the grain offering with Jesus' testimony in John 4:32-34:

> But He said to them, "I have food to eat of which you do not know." Therefore, the disciples said to one another, "Has anyone brought Him anything to eat?" Jesus, said to them, "My food is to do the will of Him who sent Me, and to finish His work."

We again see that obedience to the Father's will brings true satisfaction and fulfillment. Obedience to His will is to be our daily bread. Partaking of the Lord Himself and doing His will is the only thing that will satisfy the longing of our souls. Jesus said this was His sustenance, and it should be ours as well.

Leviticus 2:11 mentions another key word in connection with the grain offering: "honey." This is another word in the Bible that can have more than one meaning, depending on the context. Honey can be a reference to the "sweetness" of God's Word and His testimonies (Psalm 19:10), or it can be a reference to the wanton pleasures of sin, as it is apparently used here, as the Israelites are instructed to omit honey from their grain offerings.

Honey, although it is a natural sweetener, can eventually cause fermentation and decay. It represents the temporal sweetness and pleasures of worldliness (Hebrews 11:25) that will eventually ruin the "bread" of our lives. Honey also attracts flies, which are associated with disease, death, and a bad odor: *"Dead flies putrefy the perfumer's ointment, and cause it to give off a foul odor"* (Ecclesiastes 10:1a). In this way, the long-term effect of mixing honey with the offering would be to neutralize the sweet aroma of the frankincense.

The grain offering portrays the great joy that should mark the lives of God's covenant people. When we clearly see the awesome atoning work of Christ for us on the cross, we have no alternative but to break forth in great thanksgiving and joy. Let us joyously partake of Jesus—our daily bread and source of eternal sustenance.

seven

SALTY CHRISTIANS

THE GRAIN OFFERING PART 2

Through Jesus' sinless service, He became our grain offering so we might freely commune with the Father. He was sifted like fine flour, anointed with the oil of the Holy Spirit and the sweet aroma of frankincense, and found without sin (leaven) having forsaken the pleasures of the world (honey). However, the grain offering also points to Jesus as the salt of the earth who came to transform us into "salty Christians." In Christ we are to be preservatives in a dying world and flavor in a lifeless world.

Salt was a crucial element of the grain offerings, as seen in Leviticus 2:13:

> *And for every offering of your grain offering you shall season with salt; you shall not allow the salt of the covenant of your God to be lacking from your grain offering. With all your offerings you shall offer salt.*

Why the reference here to salt? Why is salt a required ingredient for every single grain offering? And what is the reference to "the salt of the covenant of your God"? Salt is obviously a very significant part of the eternal covenant which God fashioned from before the foundation of the world. Just as leaven and honey are referenced as things to *exclude* from the grain offerings, salt is mentioned as a key ingredient to *include*. Again, there is a spiritual meaning that goes beyond the mere physical attributes of salt. Yet, in order to see the spiritual meaning, it is helpful to realize salt's unique physical characteristics.

First, salt is an essential micronutrient for our bodies. Many of our internal chemical processes are dependent upon the presence of adequate amounts of salt. Without a proper intake of salt, many of our body's functions would be thrown into utter disarray. Our muscles would start cramping, and our ligaments and tendons would become brittle and lose their elasticity and strength. Eventually our bodies would begin to overheat and totally shut down due to a breakdown in our natural cooling process through perspiration.

These are just a few of the adverse reactions likely to occur in our bodies because of a lack of salt. Fortunately, God has provided salt in all types of edible plant and animal food sources, so there is seldom any worry about not getting enough salt. Yet it is important for us to see how salt is a fundamental building block of our physical makeup.

Throughout the centuries, salt has been used to preserve food and provide flavor. It has also been used in medicinal ways, as a disinfectant. Jesus spoke of salt in connection with its ability to preserve, flavor, and disinfect the surrounding culture:

> *You are the salt of the earth; but if the salt loses its flavor, how shall it be seasoned? It is then good*

for nothing but to be thrown out and trampled underfoot by men. You are the light of the world. A city that is set on a hill cannot be hidden. Nor do they light a lamp and put it under a basket, but on a lampstand, and it gives light to all who are in the house. Let your light so shine before men, that they may see your good works and glorify your Father in heaven" (Matthew 5:13-16).

In these verses, Jesus uses two primary word pictures to illustrate His desire for us to influence and impact our world: salt and light. We've often heard the saying, "You can lead a horse to water, but you can't make him drink." This is true, but you you *can* give the horse salt and make him thirsty.

Like salt, our lives should create a spiritual thirst in those around us. Our godly lifestyles should also serve as preservatives and healing agents in an evil society. Our words should serve to melt cold hearts and tenderize hearts that have hardened.

"DEAD SEA" CHRISTIANS

In the ancient world, salt had commercial value as a preservative or condiment. The primary source of salt was the area southwest of the Dead Sea. However, the impure salt from this area was susceptible to deterioration, and the salt residue often became flavorless and worthless crystals.

The Dead Sea is also known as the Salt Sea. It receives water from the Jordan River, yet has no outlet. By constantly accumulating salt sediment from the erosion of minerals in the rocks along the riverbed, the salinity of the sea has become so high that it is hostile to most plant and animal life. The sea has literally become "dead," and so it is aptly named the "Dead Sea."

There is a sobering lesson for us here. A Christian who takes in the blessings of God but never passes them on to others will eventually become stagnant and lifeless. His selfish lifestyle, like the Dead Sea, is antithetical to spiritual life. Yes, God wants to bless His people—but He does so because He wants us to be a blessing to others (Genesis 12:2).

While the salty Dead Sea was lifeless, the exact opposite is true of "salty Christians." This is the context of the Beatitudes in Matthew 5:1-16. When we allow the Lord to work through us as He teaches in the Beatitudes, we bring life and light to the world around us. But our "salt" must be pure. If it loses its purity and its flavor, it becomes good for nothing. If it loses its potency, it is unable to serve as a flavorer, preservative, healing agent, or tenderizer. This is no minor issue! Jesus warns us in Mark 9:49-50a:

> *For everyone will be seasoned with fire, and every sacrifice will be seasoned with salt. Salt is good, but if the salt loses its flavor, how will you season it?*

Without salt, our good deeds or "sacrifices" lose their value and become worthless. We who profess Christ must have a passion for Him that is greater than our desire for anything else. We need a consecrated life that allows Him to purge us—by fire and salt—of the destructive influences in our hearts. Only then will His presence rise in us in such a powerful way that the world takes notice.

THE COVENANT OF SALT

Jesus continues, *"Have salt in yourselves, and have peace with one another"* (Mark 9:50b). This calls attention to the use of salt in covenant-making. Not only is salt an effective preservative, but the Scriptures also use it as a picture of our unending covenant with God and with each other. This is referred to as a "covenant of salt" (Numbers 18:19, 2 Chronicles 13:5).

Salt, being a preservative, also helps prevent decay. Jesus, through His work on the cross, sealed an everlasting covenant with us. He has salted us with a perpetual and lasting covenant that shall keep us from the decay of sin. Our body may one day suffer decay, but our soul never will (Psalm 16:10). Jesus Himself is our "preservative." Jesus, the salt of the covenant, came to give life and flavor to our lives.

A remarkable fact about salt is that its two primary ingredients, sodium and chloride, are both poisonous! Yet, when joined together in proper proportion, these two poisons become essential nutrients for proper bodily function. While salt (sodium chloride) has great value, the separate chemical elements would kill you!

John 1:14-18 and Psalm 85:10-13 teach that Jesus is the complete and perfect balance between grace and truth, righteousness and peace. Law and truth, left to themselves, would just sentence a transgressor to death. Mercy and grace, unless anchored in the truth of God's Word, just become "cheap grace"—enabling a transgressor to deceive himself with relativism and become his own god. However, when God's mercy and truth come together, there is spiritual health and vitality.

Like sodium chloride, the scriptural combination of grace and truth brings us life. The law kills. But false grace is just as deadly. Counterfeit grace justifies by rationalization and excuse, rather than by the blood of Jesus. It makes a mockery of genuine grace and, in effect, such a person *"has trampled the Son of God underfoot, counted the blood of the covenant by which he was sanctified a common thing, and insulted the Spirit of grace ... "* (Hebrews 10:29). Jesus displayed the perfect balance between grace and truth. He came not to destroy the Law, but to fulfill it by giving His life for us on the cross (Matthew 5:17-18). True life is only available through Him!

The covenant of salt is not just a mystical theory, but rather should be reflected as a daily reality in the lives of

God's people. This has practical ramifications, such as Paul's admonition in Colossians 4:5-6 that Christians are to "season" their talk and their actions with "salt":

Walk in wisdom toward those who are outside, redeeming the time. Let your speech always be with grace, seasoned with salt, that you may know how you ought to answer each one.

These verses are a wonderful follow-up on Jesus' teaching that we are to be the salt of the earth. They are also a direct New Testament reflection of the grain offering described in Leviticus 2:13. When we offer ourselves as grain offerings of sinless service, we are to offer ourselves with "salt." This means seasoning ourselves with salt—His balanced nature of grace and truth. In so doing, everything we say or do in Jesus' name will be a demonstration of resurrection life—not a reflection of dead, legalistic Pharisaism!

So, in both the Old and New Testaments, God instructs us to be the salt of the earth. He warns us not to lose our potency, but to season everything we do, say, or think with His supernatural life. Salty Christians, infused with the life of Christ, cannot help but display fruitful lives of service. Christ in us is the only hope for preserving and revitalizing a dull and lifeless world (Colossians 1:27).

Numbers 18:19 and 2 Chronicles 13:5 teach that salt is vitally related to the concept of covenant. In ancient times, whenever two people sat down to share a covenant meal, they would always season their food with salt. This shaking of covenant salt over the meal was the event that activated, or gave life to, the covenant being established. Adding salt was the final act of consummation of that covenant. Likewise, to "activate" our covenant with God, we must trust Him to infuse us with His life. The salt of covenant points to the cross as a perpetual sign of God's eternal love, sealed by Christ's shed blood.

RESURRECTION LIFE

On the cross, Jesus paid the penalty for our sins. But the story didn't end there. If Jesus had only died and remained in the grave, all the faith in the world would not be able to save us. As wonderful as it is that Jesus died for our sins, His covenant life could not have been activated in us without the resurrection. Romans 5:10 expressly teaches that, although we are reconciled to God through the death of His Son, we are saved *through His life!* What life? His resurrection life! The power that raised Jesus from the grave is the same spiritual force that is available to give us life today! (Romans 8:9-11)

How can so many professing Christians and churches be spiritually dead today, when such overwhelming power is available to us in the Holy Spirit? Some are merely ignorant of the provisions offered in the new covenant. Incorrect theology has led many believers to expect a mediocre and powerless life. Other Christians have forfeited the benefits of the covenant because they have allowed sin to dilute their saltiness.

Many believers live in bitterness and defeat, not realizing that their covenant God offers them healing. In 2 Kings 2:19-22, Elisha employed salt as a type of the resurrection power and healing virtue available in the covenant. As salt was cast into the foul, bitter waters, a miraculous "healing" occurred and the land was no longer barren. Touched by resurrection power, the waters of death became waters of life. Jesus, who is the salt of the covenant, is also the resurrection and the life (John 11:25-26).

Without Jesus' resurrection, there would be no final consummation or "activation" of the covenant. The Christian life would be just a bundle of "DOs" and "DON'Ts," and we would be left without any power to live the life God calls us to. How is Jesus the author of a better covenant (Hebrews 8:6)? Because He not only died for our sins (as happened with the animal sacrifices in the Old Testament), but He also rose again, leaving those sins in the grave!

When the Israelites offered "salt" with their sacrificial offerings, their actions spoke prophetically of the resurrection of Jesus Christ. They were symbolically adding the crucial ingredient of resurrection life to their sacrifices—Jesus, the true salt of the covenant! Jesus heals us, preserves us, tenderizes our hearts, gives flavor to our very existence, and gives us a thirst for things of the Spirit, which He quenches Himself.

May He season us with this salt, so we may become the salt of the earth.

eight

It Is Well With My Soul

The Peace Offering Part I

True inner peace seems to be one of the rarest of human experiences. People seek it in material prosperity, but it is not found there. Alcoholics try in vain to drown their sorrows and find peace in a bottle. Others place their hope on finding the perfect sexual partner, but that kind of pleasure is always fleeting. And what about drugs, whether prescription or illegal? Yes, they are sometimes able to mimic a sense of well-being and peace, but do we really want our tranquility to be based on pills or injections?

Although we may chase for inner peace elsewhere, in Christ it is readily available to all of us who are God's covenant partners. Jesus offers a depth of serenity that has nothing to do with our outward circumstances: *"Peace I leave with you, My peace I give to you; not as the world gives do I give to you. Let not your heart be troubled, neither let it be afraid"* (John 14:27).

What does it look like to have this kind of peace that Jesus promises—peace that is not dependant upon our outward circumstances? Perhaps you have heard Horatio Spafford's timeless hymn, "It Is Well With My Soul." But few people know the amazing background of that song, an inspiring testimony of the inner peace available to us in Christ.

Born in 1828, Spafford became a successful lawyer and businessman in Chicago. He was a deeply religious man, active in his Presbyterian church as a Sunday school teacher and lay leader. Beginning in the 1870s, Spafford's faith was tested by a chain of tragic events. In 1871, the Great Chicago Fire destroyed a huge portion of the Spafford's real estate investments. In 1873, a physician counseled the Spaffords to take an extended vacation for the sake of Mrs. Spafford's health and the family's well-being.

Knowing their dear friend Dwight L. Moody would be preaching in an evangelistic tour of England, the Spaffords decided to vacation there. Spafford's wife, Anna, and their four daughters—Maggie, Tanetta, Annie, and Bessie— boarded an American ship named the *S.S. Ville du Havre.* Detained due to business, Mr. Spafford stayed behind but intended to follow his family in a few days.

On November 22, 1873, the *Ville du Havre,* sailing off the coast of Newfoundland, was struck by an English ship, the *Lochearn,* and sank in 12 minutes. Two hundred and twenty-six lives were lost, including the Spaffords' four daughters. After hours of floating in the chilly waters, Mrs. Spafford was rescued. Arriving in Wales, she cabled her husband with the short message, "Saved alone." Receiving the horrifying news, Spafford left immediately by ship to join his wife.

Spafford asked the captain of the ship to notify him when they approached the approximate area where the *Ville du Havre* went down. Notified that they were nearing the scene of his daughters' tragic deaths, Spafford went down into his cabin and penned the words to "It Is Well with My Soul." When the Spaffords eventually met up with Dwight L. Moody, Mr. Spafford told him quietly, "It is well. The will of God be done."

Spafford found an inner peace in Christ that was totally at odds with his outward situation. Look at the awesome words of this beloved hymn:

When peace, like a river, attendeth my way,
When sorrows like sea billows roll;
Whatever my lot, Thou hast taught me to say,
"It is well, it is well with my soul."
It is well with my soul
It is well, it is well with my soul.

Tho' Satan should buffet, tho' trials should come,
Let this blest assurance control,
That Christ has regarded my helpless estate,
And hath shed His own blood for my soul.
It is well with my soul
It is well, it is well with my soul.

My sin... O, the bliss of this glorious thought,
My sin, not in part but the whole,
Is nailed to the cross and I bear it no more,
Praise the Lord, praise the Lord, O my soul!
It is well with my soul
It is well, it is well with my soul.

And Lord, haste the day when the faith shall be sight,
The clouds be rolled back as a scroll,
The trump shall resound and the Lord shall descend,
"Even so" — it is well with my soul.
It is well with my soul
It is well, it is well with my soul.

I have a friend named Francis in Malaysia who is an exceptionally successful and influential businessman, heading up one of the largest conglomerates of companies in Asia, based in Kuala Lumpur. He travels easily in and out of offices of heads of state all over the world, palaces of kings and government leaders, and international summits on business and economics, yet he still takes time to reach out to the needy. He has been given the title "Tan Sri," the highest title that can be bestowed on someone in his country. Spafford's hymn is one of his favorite songs.

In 2003, over 50,000 people attended a concert sponsored by his company on the lawn of the Royal Crescent in Bath, U.K. In his address, Tan Sri honored heroes of the faith who helped shape the spiritual culture of Bath, including George Whitfield and John Wesley. He also arranged for The Three Tenors to sing, "It Is Well With My Soul."

Shortly before this book was published, Tan Sri experienced, like Spafford, a premature loss in his own life when his wife, Rose, went to be with Jesus after fighting a battle with cancer for seven years. A line of visitors and well-wishers, along with the media, stretched outside the house waiting to attend the funeral service, held at the family's home. Rose had been a vivacious, popular television personality in Hong Kong before she and Francis married, and her homeland wept at her passing. Spafford's hymn was sung at her funeral.

"When I learned about the grief sweeping Hong Kong, I began to understand that God is teaching me His ways," said Tan Sri. God continues to be his peace.

THE PEACE OFFERING

Horatio Spafford and Tan Sri both discovered the peace in Christ that is not dependent upon any earthly circumstance. This is pictured in the Old Testament as the *peace offering*, also known as the fellowship offering. This offering is a vow of friendship and a spontaneous expression of one's gratitude and commitment to God. The peace offering represents the intimate, peaceful fellowship Christians can have with the Father because of what Jesus accomplished on the cross. The result of our fellowship with God and one another through this offering is a sweet aroma of peace. There were three types of peace offerings: the *praise*, the *vow*, and the *freewill*. The Hebrew phrase for "peace offering" could be translated in various ways: fellowship offering, communion offering, shared offering, or well-being offering. Since it was appropriate to offer up a peace offering at any time, it was the most frequently offered of the sacrifices.

As we have already seen, Jesus is pictured in all of the preceding offerings. But we must also lay hold of Him as our peace offering. The cross has made a way for us to have intimate fellowship and sweet communion with God and with each other. This fellowship with the Lord, purchased for us on Calvary, is not a mediocre or second-rate kind of relationship. The Lord Jesus died to give us victory over sin and death, buying back creation's original intent that we would walk with God in the cool of the garden. Through the awesome work of the cross, we can enjoy unbroken fellowship and total well-being!

The word used for "peace" in Leviticus 3 is associated with the Hebrew noun *shalom*. Shalom is a wonderful word that includes a wide spectrum of meaning: peace, prosperity, completeness, wholeness, and well-being. It is also sometimes associated with the verb *shalam*, meaning to be **completed, ready,** to **remain healthy, unharmed,** to **make intact, complete, make restitution,** to

recompense, reward, to **restore, replace,** to **finish,** to **compensate** or to **fill up** that which is lacking. Do you see the fantastic implications of this? The presence of our Lord Jesus provides us with peace, wholeness, well-being—or whatever else may be lacking in our lives.

BECAUSE, BECAUSE, BECAUSE

It is impossible to grasp this great truth without breaking out into praise and gratitude! The peace offering thus was offered as an expression of gratitude and commitment. It was a spontaneous offering given by the free will of the worshipper. While the other offerings were to be given for particular reasons or under specific circumstances, situations, or times of day, the peace offering was simply offered at the discretion of the worshipper. It was fully based on the worshipper's personal sense of devotion and adoration to the Lord.

Do you see how precious this is? Instead of being born of compulsion or obligation, this offering speaks of a spontaneous, heartfelt love relationship with the Lord. It stems not from duty, but from choice. It flows not from the law, and not even out of need, but from grace.

We worship Him *because, because, because…*because of who He is and what He has already done, not for what we want Him to do.

Tan Sri once shared how the Lord spoke to his heart once while he had his hands raised in worship during a church service.

"Francis, why do you worship me?"

A little bit confused by the question, he answered, "I'm in church, Lord. That's what we do in church."

The still small voice of the Lord continued. "But why do you really worship me? Is it because of what I can do for you? What you can get from me?"

Suddenly, Tan Sri knew what the Lord was trying to say. Being a man of means and influence, he himself would sometimes wonder why people wanted relationship with him. Was it because of what he could for them? Was it because they wanted something from him?

In 1991 I was passing through Malaysia on my way back from ministering in Viet Nam. While there, I got a call from the Full Gospel Businessmen in Malaysia asking if I would address a group of people for one of their meetings. I humbly accepted. At this first meeting, I met a very distinguished gentleman who introduced himself and began to explain who he was and the influence he has. It was Tan Sri. I recognized quickly he was not telling me these things out of pride, but to make a point. As a young believer in Christ, he did not know who he could really trust.

While I was speaking to the group, he had felt something leap inside of him that he thought was the Holy Spirit telling him we were to connect. We have been friends now for years because of the common trust based in Christ and a common compassion for the needs of others. But even at that first meeting, I said to him: "I prefer that you not consider giving money to myself or the ministry." In the back of my mind, I thought, "Doug, why would you say this? You know the ministry has needs." But I wanted Tan Sri to know he could trust me, that I wanted to be his friend for who he was, not for what he could do for me. I wanted to be his friend, *just because*... My own life and the ministry have since benefited in ways we had not imagined, and Tan Sri has been a blessing to many others serving the Lord as well.

The Lord loves our worship and our fellowship when it is voluntary, when it is given freely. We have a volunteer who often brings her children to the office when she comes to serve. Whenever these three little girls see me, their eyes light up and they come running to greet me and hug me. It's totally spontaneous, not because of anything I do for them. They love to spend time with me, *just because* ...

That's what God wants from us, too. He wants us to come to Him spontaneously, not out of duty or compulsion. He wants us to fellowship with Him, to trust Him. He wants us to worship Him for who He is *to* us, not for what He can do *for* us.

The Lord is saying through the peace offering, "Come and enjoy fellowship with Me any time you want. My arms are always open to receive you and enjoy your heartfelt company!" God's invitation to the worshipper through the peace offering was an open-door policy. Instead of being based on complicated religious requirements, it was an open-ended invitation to come and talk, sing, laugh, cry, mourn, dance, or weep.

It's an invitation to fellowship with Him and to worship Him and to rest in His peace ... *because, because, because!*

A Move of the Spirit

There was one exception to the spontaneous and voluntary nature of the peace offerings: This offering was commanded to be included at the feast of Pentecost (Leviticus 23:19). How appropriate it is that Pentecost—eventually fulfilled by the outpouring of the Holy Spirit in Acts 2—was accompanied by sweet worship and fellowship with the Lord. This is the promised result of our intense desire to spend intimate time with God!

I had an experience that confirmed this many years ago. It was Saturday night and our ministry team was having a birthday party at the women's discipleship house we used to have. We were all pretty exhausted from various ministry activities and outreaches. I had been on a hectic travel and ministry schedule, and had just arrived back in Houston a couple of days earlier.

At one point that evening, my friend Dan looked at me and said, "Man, I really need to go home. I'm tired and I've got to get up early tomorrow to do some work." I said, "Okay," but all of a sudden I felt like singing. Seemingly out of nowhere, I began the chorus of "Our God Is an Awesome God."

At first Dan and the others looked at me as if I was crazy. It wasn't long, however, before he started singing with me. Soon, everyone began joining in with this spontaneous song of praise. It became a time of sweet worship, and before long the Holy Spirit seemed to overtake us and manifest His presence in a special way. The Lord began to supernaturally speak to each of us, encouraging us in the midst of our weariness.

As happened on that Saturday night years ago, the Spirit of God is often poured out in remarkable ways as a direct result of spontaneous worship and fellowship with God. As with the peace offering in Leviticus, when we express our love for the Lord with adoring gratitude and commitment, His presence comes to rejoice with us!

SACRIFICES OF PRAISE

One of the three types of peace offerings described in Leviticus 7:11-27 is called the *praise* or *thank offering*. This is the "sacrifice of thanksgiving" about which the psalmist speaks (Psalm 116:17, Psalm 107:22). It is also echoed in the worshipful exhortation of Psalm 100:4: *"Enter into His gates with thanksgiving, and into His courts with praise. Be thankful to Him, and bless His name."*

Whenever we enter a difficult period in our lives or become overwhelmed by stressful circumstances, the last thing we *feel* like doing is praising God. Yet that is exactly where God wants to teach us about offering this "sacrifice of praise" by faith. He inhabits the praises of His people (Psalm 22:3), and during our praises He moves on our behalf in ways we may not see, feel, or understand at the time.

A friend of mine once wrote a song called "Praise Him Through It." Regardless of what we may be going through, the Lord deserves our praise for who He is and what He has done. His heart is touched by our spontaneous praise and expressions of gratitude. When praise goes up, His glory comes down!

The second type of peace offering is the **vow offering.** This offering is intended to be a testimony of one's obedience and faith in God. After completion of a vow before the Lord, the worshipper would come to offer this sacrifice in gratitude for the grace God gave him to perform it. Our vow to completely surrender to God is a sweet-smelling offering in which He takes great delight. Many of us have broken our vows and promises to God, but the peace offering displays Jesus as our unbroken covenant of peace with God.

The third and final peace offering is the **freewill** or **voluntary offering**. This offering is characteristic of a rejoicing heart—a good heart! Ordinarily, only animals without flaw or blemish could be sacrificed. In the same way, the Lord wants to purify our hearts so we can truly worship Him. He wants our worship to flow from grateful and unblemished hearts.

But there is a much more important principle in the requirement of unblemished sacrifices. The sacrifices had to be without spot or blemish because they were prophetic types of the perfect sacrifice which Jesus became. Once and for all, the perfect Lamb of God was sacrificed in order to take away the sins of the world.

IMPERFECT BUT JOYOUS WORSHIPPERS

Leviticus 22:23 includes an intriguing exception to the usual requirement that a sacrificed animal be perfect: *"Either a bull or a lamb that has any limb too long or too short you may offer as a freewill offering ... "* What is the significance of this exception? The freewill peace offering was just that—voluntary! People who offered this sacrifice were motivated simply by their deep love for the Lord. If an animal's limb was out of proportion, God would nevertheless accept the offering because He saw the sincere motivation of the worshipper's heart.

The "blemishes" allowed in this particular peace offering are wholly typical of us—certainly not the spotless Lamb of God. But what is the message here? First and foremost, God is looking to the *heart* of the worshipper. It doesn't matter what color or race we are. Nor does it matter if we are short or tall, if we can sing or if we can't even carry a tune. These outward traits don't matter, because God looks at the worshipper's heart.

The "short limbs" referred to in Leviticus 22:23 are also a perfect picture of another important truth: Each of us is "lacking" (short) in some aspect of our relationship with God. We may desire to be living sacrifices that are "holy and acceptable to God" (Romans 12:1), yet it's only through the grace of God—through Christ Jesus, our peace offering—that we are truly acceptable in His sight.

Let's face it: In ourselves we are imperfect, blemished offerings. Our fallen nature causes us to fall short of the mark. Sin causes us to be spiritually deformed, not fit to be the kind of offering God prescribes. But there is good news! The freewill offering illustrates that we can boldly come to God by the virtue of His Son, not our own virtue. Because God sees us in His Son, He accepts us as we are.

The freewill offering was not the first sacrifice to be given, but rather was the culmination of the other offerings. The freewill offering would have been impossible if sin had not already been covered by the shedding of blood. Without Christ's great work in atoning for our sins, we could not freely give an offering of praise and thanksgiving. But now we can make a joyful noise before the Lord, and He will accept it and delight in us. What a joy to declare, "It is well with my soul!"

nine

SWEET COMMUNION

THE PEACE OFFERING PART 2

Peace, fellowship, communion, completeness, prosperity, wholeness, and well-being—these are some of the amazing benefits granted to us through Jesus, our peace offering. This truly gives us reason to rejoice and freely praise God, recommitting ourselves to the covenant we have in Christ.

In addition to being an expression of gratitude and commitment, the peace offering was a vow of *friendship*. It was a spontaneous freewill act, born of the worshipper's intense desire to fellowship with God.

Everyone yearns for true peace and well-being, but few people realize where those qualities can be found. Is the answer in more material goods? Of course not. Is well-being just a matter of having a good job or some great friends? No, for as wonderful as any outward experience may be, it is only transitory unless it is based on Christ Jesus and His eternal covenant. Lasting peace and well-being will come only from genuine communion with the Lord.

Again, Leviticus offers some fantastic insights about this sweet communion:

*When his offering is a sacrifice of a peace offering,
if he offers it of the herd, whether male or female,
he shall offer it without blemish before the LORD.
And he shall lay his hand on the head of his
offering, and kill it at the door of the tabernacle
of meeting; and Aaron's sons, the priests, shall
sprinkle the blood all around on the altar. Then
he shall offer from the sacrifice of the peace
offering an offering made of fire to the LORD. The
fat that covers the entrails and all the fat that is
on the entrails, the two kidneys and the fat that
is on them by the flanks, and the fatty lobe
attached to the liver above the kidneys, he shall
remove; and Aaron's sons shall burn it on the
altar upon the burnt sacrifice, which is on **the
wood that is on the fire**, as an offering made
by fire, a **sweet aroma** to the LORD* (Leviticus
3:1-5).

In verse five we see that the peace offering was made
after the burnt offering. Do you see the significance of that?
True peace or fellowship with God comes after surrendering
to His will. We may look for gimmicks or shortcuts to find
this kind of well-being, but we are wasting our time if we
haven't first surrendered ourselves fully to the Lord.

Verse five indicates an intriguing progression of steps to
make a peace offering. There was first the *wood* on the
altar, then the *burnt offering*, and, finally, the *peace offering*
itself. Though there is much imagery in Scripture concerning
"wood," the main significance here is that wood depicts
redemption, *restoration*, and *judgment*. Jesus, our burnt
offering, was laid upon the wood of the cross, being
exposed, shamed, and judged for our sins. On the wood of
the cross, He became our perfect burnt offering.

For the joy that was set before Him, Jesus was obedient

to the point of death (Hebrews 12:2-3, Philippians 2:8). In so doing, He became our grain offering of sinless service, through which we have peace, fellowship, and communion with God. Our redemption and restoration are the direct result of the high cost He paid for us on "the wood"—the cross. The altar and wood in the Old Testament sacrificial system were a type of the cross in the New Testament. As the fire consumed the sacrifices, so did the fire of God's judgment consume our sins through our Lord Jesus.

JESUS, CENTER OF EVERYTHING

By now a startling truth should be evident: Jesus is the theme in every verse of the Old Testament law! He is the literal, physical fulfillment of the Old Testament types and shadows. All of our faith, hope, and love can be safely placed in Him, for He is the theme of it all! That's why Jesus could challenge the religious leaders of His day: *"You search the Scriptures, for in them you think you have eternal life; and these are they which testify of Me"* (John 5:39).

Leviticus 3:11 contains another staggering prophetic type. Here, as well as in Leviticus 7:11-27, we see parts of the peace offering referred to as the "food" of the offering. The peace offering was the only sacrifice in which the person making the offering received anything back from what he presented. Both the person bringing the offering and the priest got to eat from the offering. This represents mutual acceptance and mutual enjoyment between man, priest, and God. At the peace offering they communed together—fellowship made possible through the blood covenant that gave them a common bond.

The peace offering was also offered with a grain offering (Leviticus 7:12-13), and the grain offering was accompanied by a drink offering, which was made of wine (Leviticus 23:13,18). Do you seeing anything significant here? The combination of these offerings represented *bread* and *wine*! Here, in the grandeur of the Old Testament sacrifice system, we have a beautiful picture of Holy Communion, which Jesus Himself instituted shortly before His death. Hundreds of years before Jesus' passion on the cross, the peace offering testified of the sweet fellowship and communion with God provided by Jesus through the new covenant.

PURGING THE LEAVEN

The peace offering is to be undertaken in the spirit of humble thanksgiving and gratitude of heart. The unleavened bread and finely blended flour, mixed with oil, speak of fellowship or communion that is void of wrong motives and sin (Leviticus 7:12). How can we invite the presence of God into our churches, homes, families, marriages, or friendships, if we are unwilling to get rid of the "leaven" in our character, which is so displeasing to the Lord? If the presence and power of the Holy Spirit are conspicuously absent from our lives, we may need to take inventory of what the hindrances may be.

In many cases, the issue of leaven is one of spiritual pride. Just as yeast (leaven) causes bread to rise, so pride tends to "puff us up." Paul warned the Corinthians that they needed to be careful that their spiritual knowledge didn't lead to this kind of pride: *"Knowledge puffs up, but love edifies [builds up]"* (1 Corinthians 8:1). He also told the Corinthians:

> *Your glorying is not good. Do you not know that a little leaven leavens the whole lump? Therefore purge out the old leaven, that you may be a new lump, since you truly are unleavened. For indeed Christ, our Passover, was sacrificed for us. Therefore let us keep the feast, not with old leaven, nor with the leaven of malice and wickedness,*

but with the unleavened bread of sincerity and truth (1 Corinthians 5:6-8).

Referring back to the Old Testament Feast of Unleavened Bread, Paul challenged the Corinthians to purge their pride, malice, and wickedness. Certainly the same message is needed in the church today. The peace offering beckons us to a wonderful new level of communion with the Lord and each other, but this is only possible after we rid our hearts of leaven.

James 3:13-14 provides a graphic description of the devastating effect leaven has on our relationships:

> *Who is wise and understanding among you? Let him show by good conduct that his works are done in the meekness of wisdom. But if you have bitter envy and self-seeking [selfish ambition] in your hearts, do not boast and lie against the truth.*

When we "lie against the truth," we are, in effect, resisting the lordship of Christ in our lives. Lying is a satanic tool for getting what we want. If we are more concerned about pleasing ourselves than about serving others, then bitterness, envy, strife, and confusion will be the result. James continues:

> *This wisdom does not descend from above, but is earthly, sensual, demonic. For where envy and self-seeking exist, confusion and every evil thing are there* (James 3:15-16).

How many times have we, out of our opinionated desire to get our own way, accused others and unwittingly initiated strife? When we engage in such activities, we put ourselves in league with satan, "the accuser of our brethren" (Revelation 12:10). Our lusts and selfishness turn us into tools of the enemy to destroy and divide our brothers and sisters in Christ. Leaven in our hearts opens us up to confusion and "every evil work."

However, James also shows an encouraging glimpse at the wisdom that flows from "unleavened" hearts:

> *But the wisdom that is from above is first pure, then peaceable, gentle, willing to yield, full of mercy and good fruits, without partiality and without hypocrisy. Now the fruit of righteousness is sown in peace by those who make peace* (James 3:17-18).

The peace offering—reflecting fellowship that is a sweet aroma to God—is characterized by this type of wisdom. We are to be *peacemakers*, not strife-makers! Our peaceful fellowship should foster wholeness, completeness, and prosperity.

Why do people sometimes harbor bitterness, envy, and strife in their hearts? James says this condition is earthly, sensual, and devilish. Leaven of this sort is a cancer to our fellowship with God and with one another. A little leaven of this kind can indeed leaven the whole lump of dough!

God wants His children to love one another and to walk in unity, so that His presence and anointing might flow through our lives in an unrestricted way. Christ-like fellowship releases God's blessings:

> *Behold, how good and how pleasant it is for brethren to dwell together in unity!...For there the* LORD *commands the blessing...* (Psalm 133:1-3).

Our motives, our thankfulness, our respect, our love, and our appreciation for one another all have a bearing on this corporate anointing. We should regard our fellowship as a type of communion. We are each part of the Lord's body. We should extend the gracious heart attitude of the peace offering to each other, just as it has been extended to us by Christ (Romans 15:7).

The apostle Peter had a special gift and passion for winning the lost, but he also realized that outreach would be hindered if believers failed in their responsibility to love each other: *"And above all things have fervent love for one another, for 'love will cover a multitude of sins'"* (1 Peter 4:8). *"Be diligent to be found by Him in peace, without spot and blameless"* (2 Peter 3:14b).

Jesus, our peace offering, desires for us to diligently seek Him, manifesting His covenant of peace through us to a needy world. May we come before Him with spontaneous adoration, praise, and thanksgiving for what He has already done. May we renew our vow to covenant relationship with Him and with one another, enjoying the full extent of our fellowship and sweet communion with our Lord.

ten

JESUS: OUR EXPUNGER, OUR PURIFIER AND OUR GUILT-BEARER

THE SIN OFFERING PART I

The words from a familiar chorus say it well: "We owed a debt we could not pay; He paid a debt He did not owe." We owed a debt—a huge debt of sin, which we had no way to repay. Though He did not owe us anything, Jesus graciously paid this debt for us.

The **sin offering** depicts Christ as our *expunger, purifier,* and *guilt-bearer.* Like a refiner's fire that causes impurities to surface so the dross can be removed, Jesus purifies us until we become precious gems and valuable treasure. Motivated by pure love, He stepped forward to pay our debt in full, though He Himself was sinless.

The sin offering is a beautiful picture of Christ as our guilt-bearer, the One who secured the forgiveness of our sins. He came as the Lamb of God, who takes away the sin of the world (John 1:29). He took the place we deserved— the place of condemnation and death—and exchanged His righteousness for our unrighteousness.

Some people think God is like a kindly old man in the sky who just winks at the sins we commit. Yes, God is a God of love, but He also demands perfect justice. Sins can't just be covered over or ignored, they must be fully expunged and atoned for. The dictionary definition of "expunge" is "to erase or strike out; to eliminate completely; to annihilate." Do you see how accurately this describes the complete purging of our sins?

Several years ago, a woman who became a part of our ministry had at one time been arrested with false charges of lewd behavior. The charges were dropped but the arrest remained on her record. As she grew in the Lord, she began pursuing a call God placed on her heart to be a nurse. She went to a local community college, where she excelled as a student. But before she applied for nursing school, she feared being rejected because of the arrest. With the help of a Christian attorney, we were able to have the arrest expunged from her record, and she was accepted into nursing school as though the incident never existed!

This is what Jesus does for us: He expunges our sins, wipes our record clean, and redeems our mistakes!

INADVERTENT AND IGNORANT SINS

The **sin offering** (also known as the guilt or purification offering) was offered to make atonement for sins, whether intentional or unintentional. Why would expunging and expiation be needed for inadvertent sins or acts of negligence and failure? In such cases, there may not have been a blatant breaking of God's commandments, but a defilement or breach of relationship occurred nevertheless.

The explanation of the sin offering in Leviticus 4 is the longest of all the descriptions of sacrificial offerings. This is indicative of the depth to which it impacts lives. The chapter begins:

And the LORD spoke to Moses, saying... "If a person sins unintentionally [i.e., through error or ignorance] against any of the commandments of the Lord in anything which ought not to be done, and does any of them..." (Leviticus 4:1-2).

Again and again, the chapter refers to those who sin unintentionally, by error or ignorance. Repetition in Scripture is like a flashing neon sign. Whenever the Lord repeats a certain phrase over and over again, He is trying to get our attention! For example, in Psalm 136 we are repeatedly reminded that God's mercy endures forever. God doesn't want us to miss the point!

So what does it mean to sin "unintentionally"? This refers to sins done in ignorance, where the guilty party did not realize his act was wrong. But why is there a specific offering for sins done in ignorance? Often we unintentionally break the commandments of God just by "missing the mark." But when the Holy Spirit shows us our error, we should be quick to acknowledge and repent of our misguided ways.

Likewise, the sin offering in Leviticus depicts a person who has become aware of his inadvertent sin: *"...if his sin which he has committed comes to his knowledge, he shall bring as his offering a kid of the goats, a male without blemish"* (Leviticus 4:23). In a rather matter-of-fact way, the person who sins unintentionally is simply told to bring a sin offering. That's the end of the issue.

However, there is a vast distinction between this type of ignorant misdeed and a willful, intentional act of rebellion against the Lord. Hebrews 10:26 warns: *"For if we sin **willfully** after we have received the **knowledge of the truth**, there no longer remains a sacrifice for sins."* The warning continues a few verses later:

Of how much worse punishment, do you suppose,

will he be thought worthy who has trampled the Son of God underfoot, counted the blood of the covenant by which he was sanctified a common thing, and insulted the Spirit of grace? (Hebrews 10:29)

Sin is a serious matter! Yes, God is gracious, but may we never get the idea that He just winks at our sins. It's one thing if our misstep is merely in ignorance, but the consequences are quite different when we habitually or willfully choose to disobey. In so doing, we trample underfoot the Son of God, dishonor His shed blood, and insult the Spirit of Grace. This is a sobering message!

Although Hebrews is a book of great encouragement, it also contains some grave warnings. The writer lists six specific hindrances to personal and corporate transformation:

1. The danger of **negligence** (Hebrews 2:1-3)

2. The danger of **hardening the heart** (Hebrews 3:7-10)

3. The danger of **unbelief** (Hebrews 3:11-12)

4. The danger of **dullness of hearing** (Hebrews 5:11-14)

5. The danger of **resisting God** (Hebrews 10:26-29)

6. The danger of **refusing Him when He speaks** (Hebrews 12:25-27)

Similar warnings are given by James, who picks up on the same distinction between sins of ignorance and intentional sins: *"Therefore, to him who **knows** to do good and does not do it, to him it is sin"* (James 4:17). And our Lord Jesus warned that those who have heard His words have no excuse for their sins: *"If I had not come and spoken* *to them, they would have no sin, but now they have **no** excuse for their sin"* (John 15:22; also see Luke 12:47-48).

JESUS, OUR GUILT-BEARER

The sin offering clearly illustrates our need for Jesus as our guilt-bearer. Paul reminded the Colossians how Jesus *"wiped out the handwriting of requirements that was against us, which was contrary to us. And He has taken it out of the way, having nailed it to the cross"* (Colossians 2:14). The sin offering is also a purification offering. Our sins are expunged, taken away, blotted out. There is literally a "de-sinning" of the altar of our hearts.

The sin offering points to many lessons that are crucial for a healthy Christian life. Jesus, our sin offering, makes atonement for our sins of ignorance—the unintentional error of our ways—for which restitution is not possible on our own (Leviticus 4:5-12). This offering portrays expiation for our inadvertent sins, negligence, and failures. When we realize some specific sin we have committed (Leviticus 4:23), we are to immediately bring it before the Lord, receiving the forgiveness paid for through Christ's work on the cross.

It is interesting that the sin offering is the first offering where **atonement** (a price being paid for sin) and **forgiveness** are mentioned in the same context: *... the priest shall make atonement ... and it shall be forgiven ...* (Leviticus 4:20, 4:26, 4:31, 4:35). The blood of bulls and goats could not permanently atone for our sins, but faith in Jesus—the perfect sacrifice and the completion of our sin offering—does (see Hebrews 8-10).

How wonderful to see the restoration of the image of God in us! Scripture proclaims that *"old things have passed away; behold, all things have become new"* (2 Corinthians 5:17). Though the Old Testament sin offering was only a foreshadow of this fantastic transformation, it still pointed to an important truth: The people of the Old Testament had to come to a genuine heart-knowledge of God, even as we do. It is one thing to serve the Lord out of form and ritual, but quite another to take the commandments and teachings of God "to heart."

Now is a good time for us to pause and ask ourselves whether we have truly appropriated the marvelous provisions illustrated in the sin offering. Jesus has done His part, perfectly fulfilling His role as our expunger, purifier, and guilt-bearer. Yet, sadly, through ignorance, unbelief, or disobedience, we often forfeit the pardon and peace that can be ours.

Lord, thank you for Your great work on our behalf! Open our eyes to see the full blessings that can be ours!

eleven

PURITY, PASSION AND PURPOSE

THE SIN OFFERING PART II

Now that we have some understanding regarding the central theme of the sin offering, let's look at how it relates to four specific categories of people: the priest (Leviticus 4:3-12), the whole congregation (Leviticus 4:13-21), a ruler (Leviticus 4:22-26), or any one of the common people (Leviticus 4:27-35).

For various reasons, the Lord makes a distinction between these different categories and in the type of animal specified for the offering. We also see differing levels of responsibility.

THE PRIEST

Leviticus first describes how the sin offering applies to an "anointed priest":

> *If the anointed priest sins, bringing guilt on the people, then let him offer to the Lord for his sin which he has sinned a young bull without blemish as a sin offering* (Leviticus 4:3).

The principle here is pretty apparent. As we see throughout the Scriptures, judgment begins with the priest and with the house of the Lord. The priest who sinned was required to bring a young bull for a sin offering. So if a priest lied, cheated, stole, or committed some other offense, he was held accountable before God just like anyone else. One difference we find in the offering of the priest was the type of animal required for the sacrifice. While any animal without blemish would generally be expensive (sin costs!), young bulls and rams were usually the most expensive offerings of all. Goats and lambs were the next most costly, and turtledoves and pigeons were the cheapest.

Why was the priest required to bring the most valuable and expensive type of animal? Because he carried a higher level of accountability before the Lord. Jesus taught His disciples that to whom much is given, much will be required (Luke 12:48). Since the priest was called to be a reflection of God's holiness, he had to pay a higher price for his sin. James echoed this warning to those who would be leaders in the church: *"My brethren, let not many of you become teachers, knowing that we shall receive a stricter judgment"* (James 3:1).

Judgment starts within the house of the Lord (1 Peter 4:17). As the leaders go, so go the people. Look again at verse 3: ***"If the anointed priest sins, bringing guilt on the people ..."*** When God begins to "clean house," He begins with the leadership. Perhaps leaders are worthy of double honor (1 Timothy 5:17), but they also receive double judgment!

The prophet Malachi spoke of a day when the Lord will send His messenger to prepare a way before Him and cleanse His temple. Notice that "the sons of Levi" (i.e., the priests and leaders) are a particular focus of this fierce cleansing process:

"Behold, I send My messenger, and he will prepare the way before Me. And the Lord, whom you seek, will suddenly come to His temple, even the Messenger of the covenant, in whom you delight. Behold, He is coming," says the LORD *of hosts.*

But who can endure the day of His coming? And who can stand when He appears? For He is like a refiner's fire and like launderer's soap. He will sit as a refiner and a purifier of silver; **He will purify the sons of Levi, and purge them as gold and silver, that they may offer to the** LORD **an offering in righteousness** (Malachi 3:1-3).

Though we can see many parallels here about the refining of those who are leaders in ministry, it is good to remember that through Christ we are *all* part of the royal priesthood (1 Peter 2:9). Because of this awesome fact, we all have a responsibility to represent Christ with integrity and honor, serving as His royal ambassadors (2 Corinthians 5:20). How can God rightfully judge a world that does not know Him until He first deals with the sin of those who claim to know Him? As children of God, we are called to be examples to the world of the saving grace and mercy of the Lord. However, if we are living no differently than the children of the devil, how will they ever see their need for Christ?

Leviticus 4:4-12 offers a number of specific foreshadows of the person and work of Jesus our Messiah. In verse 4, we see the doctrine of identification. Just as the priest laid his hand upon the head of the sacrificial animal in order to transfer the sins he had committed, so must we identify with Jesus at the foot of the cross. Just as verse 4 speaks of "the door of the tabernacle," so does the "door" of Jesus' cross open our way into the presence of the Father!

Leviticus 4:5-6 moves on to provide a prophetic type of Jesus bringing His precious blood to the Father as payment for our sin (see Hebrews 8-10). The priest sprinkled the blood of the bull *seven times*—the number of perfect fulfillment—before the veil of the sanctuary. In the same way, Jesus presented His precious blood before the Father.

The veil represented a barrier to the presence of God. When Jesus' body was broken, torn, and bruised for our sakes, the barrier was forever broken. As His blood was shed for us, the veil of the temple was torn from top to bottom, providing us with complete access to the throne room of God (see Hebrews 10:17-22, Matthew 27:51).

Leviticus 4:7 speaks of the priest putting some of the sacrificial blood "on the horns of the **altar of sweet incense** before the Lord." This altar of incense represents the prayers Jesus offered, and continues to offer, on our behalf (Hebrews 13:10-16, Hebrews 5:7). It also represents the prayers of the saints that are offered in His name (Revelation 8:3).

It is significant that the blood was applied by the priest on the "**horns**" of the altar, because horns represented a place of *power* and *authority*. By the authority of the precious name of Jesus, we pray and have bold access to the throne of God. As the priest applied blood to the earthly altar of incense, so did Jesus apply His own blood to the heavenly altar of incense. This gives us *power in His name* to petition the Father.

Leviticus 4:7 continues: *"... and he shall pour the remaining blood of the bull at the base of the altar of the burnt offering, which is at the door of the tabernacle of meeting."* Jesus' blood was poured out on our behalf at the foot of the "altar of the cross." Wow! Jesus and the work of the cross are pictured in every jot and tittle of the Levitical sacrifices.

Leviticus 3:16 and 4:8-10 contain another intriguing principle: *"All the fat is the Lord's."* Why in the world would God say that He wants the *fat* of the sacrificed animals? He wants to take all that is unhealthy for us—whether sin, sickness, or disease—and take it upon Himself on the altar of the cross. Leviticus 4:10 says the fat should be put on the altar as a burnt offering. The reference to "burning" means that He judged (i.e., burned) our sin at the cross, forever attaining victory over it.

Verse 12 says that the bull should be carried "**outside the camp**," where the priest was to "burn it on wood [cf. the cross] with fire." This is a beautiful picture of Jesus being taken outside the city of Jerusalem and crucified (Hebrews 13:10-13). Although the Levitical pattern was to take the bull to "**a clean place**" where the ashes could be poured out (Leviticus 4:12), by the time of Jesus' day the clean place had become the town dump. This putrid ash heap was indicative of the spiritual state of Israel at the time.

The poured-out ashes were meant to serve as physical evidence that a redemptive sacrifice had been made and accepted by God on our behalf! However, what should have been reserved as a holy ("clean") place, by Jesus' day had been polluted by all kinds of unclean elements. Whether this redemptive place had been contaminated by garbage, dead bodies (e.g., "Place of a Skull," Matthew 27:33), or some other pollutants, Jesus' sacrifice forever made us clean in God's eyes.

It is significant in verses 8 and 9 that the animal's organs ("entrails") were burned along with the fat upon the altar of burnt offerings. However, the "body" of the bull was taken away and burned outside the camp. The reason for this was two-fold. The burning of these inner body parts teaches us that a surrendered heart precedes restoration from the effects of sin on our lives. Remember the lesson of the burnt sacrifice? A burnt offering is the place of total surrender to the Father's will. Thus, the burnt offering was made first, in order to show the contrite condition of the heart (Psalm 51). This preceded the sin offering, which was made for the actual atonement of the sin.

Second, it is important to note that the **liver** and the **kidneys** are particularly singled out to be burned in this offering (Leviticus 4:9). What is special about these particular organs? Both of them are responsible for cleansing impurities and toxins from the body. The liver especially cleanses and purifies the blood, which in turn is enabled to carry vital nourishment to every cell in our bodies. Without this cleansing and purifying process, we would surely die. If the functions of the liver and kidneys are hampered in any way, dangerous toxins accumulate. This will lead to *death* if not remedied.

The liver and kidneys being burned on the altar of burnt offering is a wonderful picture of Jesus' love for us. He totally emptied Himself and poured out His life so that He might "filter" our sin-sick blood and heal us forevermore. Jesus acts as a spiritual "liver" and "kidney" to cleanse and purify our lives from sin. What an example of His amazing love for us! Just as nothing can replace the function of our liver and kidneys, nothing can substitute for the passion of Christ on our behalf.

THE WHOLE CONGREGATION

The instructions about the sin offering continue in verse 13: *"Now if the whole congregation of Israel sins unintentionally..."* (see Leviticus 4:13-21). Although the basic ritual for the sin offering remains the same here, there are some unique points that relate to this particular class of people.

How could the entire congregation of Israel commit a sin

of ignorance? One example is the incident of the golden calf at the foot of Mount Sinai in Exodus 32. Moses was up on the mountain meeting with God, and his return was delayed.

The people felt a great spiritual need to worship "something," and in their impatience they made their own god and proclaimed, *"This is your god, O Israel, that brought you out of the land of Egypt!"* (Exodus 32:4b) Not having yet received the commandments of God, in their ignorance and impatience, they all became guilty of sin.

We might think their idolatry was quite strange and foolish, yet I have to admit that I have done virtually the same thing in my own life at times. I have grown impatient while waiting on the Lord and have "taken matters into my own hands." Instead of trusting that His ways are higher than mine, I acted as if I knew best. I inadvertently served the god of my own way.

Perhaps a better example of corporate sins of ignorance is found in 2 Kings 22. Hilkiah the high priest discovers the Book of the Law while serving in the temple, which he gives to Shaphan the Scribe. When Shaphan reads the book to King Josiah, the king tears his clothes in repentance, realizing the many laws that have been transgressed by the people:

> ... *great is the wrath of the Lord against us, because our fathers have not obeyed the words of this book, to do according to all that is written concerning us* (2 Kings 22:13).

The Book of the Law had been buried away. No one had been taught its precepts, so the entire nation, in its ignorance, had been inadvertently and corporately sinning.

Leviticus 4:14 specifies "a young bull" as the type of animal to be used for this category of sin offering. Again we see that a high price was set for this particular class of people who ignorantly departed from the commandments of God. Where there is corporate sin, much damage is done, requiring a costly atonement. Throughout Scripture, a bull or ox typifies the "suffering servant." As we have already seen, Jesus Himself was the Suffering Servant for our sakes. We, too, as a royal priesthood and holy nation, should be servants to a hurting world.

THE RULER

The next type of person addressed by the sin offering was "a ruler" (see Leviticus 4:22-26). Rulers of Israel who sinned unintentionally were required to bring a male goat without blemish. The commoner had to bring a female goat. This shows how the leader was more accountable and his restitution more costly.

There are many biblical examples of a ruler sinning: **Aaron** in the episode of the golden calf (Exodus 32); **Eli** regarding his inability to discipline his sons (1 Samuel 2:22-36); **Saul** regarding his impulsive act of offering a sacrifice (1 Samuel 13:8-14) and his failure to destroy all of the Amalekites (1 Samuel 15); and **David** regarding his adultery with Bathsheba and the murder of her husband (2 Samuel 11 and 12).

It is sobering that David, despite his tremendous heart for the Lord, did not acknowledge his error until Nathan the prophet came and exposed the deception of his heart. However, when David saw his sin, he tore his clothes and sincerely repented before God for what he had done. Broken and contrite, he begged God for forgiveness and restoration (see Psalm 51).

God heard David's repentant cry and restored him to a full relationship. It is important to remember, however, that there were still *consequences* for this ruler's sin (2 Samuel 12:8-23). Although a sad and tragic story of the deceitfulness of sin, this incident in the life of David is also a wonderful reminder of God's unfailing love, mercy, and forgiveness when we are truly broken and contrite of heart.

THE COMMON PEOPLE

The final category of people delineated for the sin offering occurs in Leviticus 4:27-35. This passage focuses on the average person—you and I. Hard as we might try, we regularly "miss the mark"! We sin against God, either by wholeheartedly rejecting His commandments or by unintentionally falling short of His best for our lives.

The animal specified for the sin offering here is a kid of the goats, a female without blemish. This seems to be a reflection of Jesus' mother, Mary. She was a virgin, a female without blemish. She was also a "commoner," and from her womb was born Jesus, the Lamb of God.

The female gender in the Bible is commonly associated with the mercy and grace of God. A father in a home typically wields the law. When a son or daughter transgresses his commandments, correction and instruction are brought. A mother, on the other hand, typically pleads for mercy on behalf of the child who has transgressed. Therefore, the unblemished female goat mentioned in Leviticus 4:28 is reflective of God's mercy and grace in the forgiveness of our sins. Yes, as a Father, God commands us to repent (Acts 17:30). But His heart is always gracious and redemptive. John 3:16 says it so beautifully: *"For God so loved the world that He gave His only begotten Son, that whoever believes in Him should not perish but have everlasting life."*

THE HELMET, THE SWORD, AND THE FIRE

If we truly see the great truths of the sin offering, we will gain a new understanding of our position in Christ. This knowledge becomes our "helmet of salvation"

(Ephesians 6:17), protecting us from any blow of the enemy. This foundation is crucial to making us strong in the faith, ever growing in our relationship with the Lord. When believers become spiritually paralyzed through insecurity, doubt, and fear, it is a sure sign they have not received the benefits of this wonderful helmet.

It is impossible to have a renewed mind unless we are willing to study and believe the Scriptures. One word from God, received at the appropriate time, can transform our lives. We desperately need the spiritual surgery only the Word of God can perform: *"For the word of God is living and powerful, and sharper than any two-edged sword, piercing even to the division of soul and spirit, and of joints and marrow, and is a discerner of the thoughts and intents of the heart"* (Hebrews 4:12). Are we willing to let God's Word do this awesome work in our hearts?

Many Christians in America today are biblically illiterate. We want the benefits of a relationship with God, complete with spiritual goose bumps and the "warm fuzzies" of spirituality. However, we have failed to embrace the power of God's Word to heal us, sustain us, and transform our character. We get upset with God for not doing more in our lives, but the truth is that we have not fully *given Him* our lives.

God is getting ready to send His fire to the earth. But we must remember that fire can either destroy or bring revival. It will burn up the dross and fluff of modern Christianity, but will ignite the hearts of those who sincerely ask God to make them living sacrifices.

The fire is coming! But don't forget: When we ask God to send His fire of revival, we cannot negotiate with the flames when they come! The same fire that ushers in revival will also bring judgment, spiritual refining, and purification. Are you ready?

twelve

PAYMENT FOR THE
DAMAGES OF SIN

THE TRESPASS OFFERING

The sin offering, discussed in the previous chapter, revealed the awesome grace of God that expunges, blots out, and wipes away the debt of our sins. While that offering deals with atonement and forgiveness, there is still another issue. The **trespass offering** deals with the *damage* caused by our sins, including damage caused to others.

Some translations call the trespass offering a "guilt offering," while others use that designation for the sin offering. While sin is "missing the mark"—willfully or unintentionally— and guilt is the consequence of sin, the rituals for both the sin and the trespass offerings were exactly the same, except for two things. In the trespass offering, the sin offering was always accompanied by a burnt offering (Leviticus 5:10) and an estimated value was paid to make amends for the harm that was done (Leviticus 5:15-16, 6:4-6).

Although the standard sin offering was given by the worshipper to make atonement where restitution was not feasible, the trespass offering was made for unintentional or lesser offenses where restitution *was* possible. In the sin offering, Jesus is our guilt-bearer. In the trespass offering, Jesus also covers the damage caused by our trespasses and sins.

How can sin's damage be repaired? It is significant that the trespass offering is the first offering to introduce the concepts of *confession, repentance,* and *restoration* (Leviticus 5:5, 5:14-19 and 6:4-7). These are the foundation for repairing the damaged caused by sin. We can see a New Testament equivalent of the trespass offering in 1 John 1:8-10:

> *If we say that we have no sin, we deceive ourselves, and the truth is not in us.* ***If we confess our sins, He is faithful and just to forgive our sins and to cleanse us from all unrighteousness.*** *If we say that we have not sinned, we make Him a liar, and His word is not in us.*

Biblical restoration of relationship involves three distinct concepts, all of which are demonstrated in the teaching of the trespass offering:

1. Confession. There must be an acknowledgment or confession of sin (Leviticus 5:5). Unless a person understands that he or she has sinned, the restoration process never gets off the ground.

2. Repentance. Along with confession of sin, there must be a true heart of repentance. Confession of sin is not genuine unless there is also repentance from that sin. It would do no good to agree with God that we have sinned unless we are also willing to undergo a change of heart. Repentance literally is defined as a change of heart that enables us to turn from sin and walk by His grace into righteousness.

3. Restoration. The final concept behind the biblical

healing of relationships is the restoration of any damage the sin has caused (Leviticus 5:14-19, 6:4-7). Confession and repentance deal more with the spiritual aspects of relationship, whereas restoration deals more with the practical aspects. The sincerity of our confession and repentance is shown by our desire to restore the loss and heal the hurts our action has caused. Whether it is by a heartfelt apology, a specific deed, or some kind of material remuneration, our actions show the sincerity of our repentance and provide recompense for the damage done.

These three components of restored relationship are paralleled in the offering rituals. The sin offering communicates an acknowledgement or confession of sin. The burnt offering portrays true, heartfelt repentance from that sin. The payment of restitution exhibits the sincerity of the repentance and is an effort to bring about tangible restoration of any hurt or damage caused by the trespass.

Leviticus 5:16 specifies that, in addition to restitution for the loss, the offending party should add a penalty of one-fifth (20 percent) of the value:

> *And he shall make restitution for the harm that he has done in regard to the holy thing, and shall add one-fifth to it and give it to the priest. So the priest shall make atonement for him with the ram of the trespass offering, and it shall be forgiven him.*

The offender had to do more than just pay back the loss—he had to pay a penalty for his action. This is a reminder that even though our sins are forgiven, our actions have practical consequences.

One of the key features of the trespass offering is that it involves *responsibility*. When we realize that we have wronged God or another person, we become responsible to do whatever we can to make things right. In contrast, Jesus was sinless and thus had no responsibility to restore a broken relationship. Yet He poured out His very own blood to cover the damage created by our sin. He laid down His life to bridge the gap between a holy God and sinful humanity. Yes, sin separates. But because Jesus became our trespass offering, we do not have to stay separated from God when we fall short of His glory.

RESTORED RELATIONSHIPS

Sin not only breaks our relationship with God—it can also separate us from other people. When we sin against someone, an invisible spiritual barrier goes up between us. Yet, here again, the work of the cross provides the remedy we need. Just as the cross reconciles us to God, it also offers restoration of our broken relationships with others.

Look at the beautiful way the cross of Christ bridged the chasm between Jews and Gentiles—a chasm which seemed totally impossible to surmount:

> *For He Himself is our **peace**, who has made both one, and has **broken down the middle wall of separation**, having abolished in His flesh the enmity, that is, the law of commandments contained in ordinances, so as to create in Himself one new man from the two, thus making **peace**, and that He might **reconcile** them both to God in one body **through the cross**, thereby putting to death the enmity. And He came and preached **peace** to you who were afar off and to those who were near. For through Him we both have access by one Spirit to the Father. Now, therefore, you are no longer strangers and foreigners, but fellow citizens with the saints and **members of the household of God** ...* (Ephesians 2:14-19).

Paul repeatedly encourages the Ephesians regarding the peace that is available to them in Christ—peace with God and peace with people. Even where seriously breached relationships have existed in the past (like the breach between Jews and Gentiles), Christ is able to break down "the middle wall of separation." Our trespasses toward each other may cause serious damage physically, emotionally, or spiritually. But the trespass offering speaks of God's desire to heal the damage through confession, repentance, and restoration.

If our relationships remain broken, it's not God's fault! There is human responsibility involved as well. Jesus repeatedly challenges us that we must *forgive* each other when we have been wronged. In the Lord's Prayer, He tells us to pray, *"And forgive us our debts [trespasses], as we forgive our debtors [those who trespass against us]"* (Matthew 6:12). A few verses later He adds a sobering warning: *"For if you forgive men their trespasses, your heavenly Father will also forgive you. But if you do not forgive men their trespasses, neither will your Father in Heaven forgive your trespasses"* (Matthew 6:14-15).

If the message on forgiveness wasn't already clear enough, Jesus later tells a story about a man who was forgiven a huge debt, then refused to forgive someone else a very small debt. Upon hearing this, the man's master (who had forgiven him the huge debt) became very angry:

> *Then his master, after he had called him, said to him, "You wicked servant! I forgave you all that debt because you begged me. Should you not also have had compassion on your fellow servant, just as I had pity on you?" And his master was angry, and **delivered him to the torturers** until he should pay all that was due to him. So My heavenly Father also will do to you if each of you,*

*from his heart, does not forgive his brother his
trespasses* (Matthew 18:21-35).

Oh, the untold torment people undergo because they
have not learned to forgive! If God can forgive us for all we
have done against Him, we certainly have no right to
withhold forgiveness from each other!

THE CURE FOR SIN'S CONSEQUENCES

What took place on the cross 2000 years ago was most
holy in the sight of God. Jesus became the perfect sacrifice
for our sin. He became our trespass offering, so now He can
offer healing for the damage brought about by our sins. In
one moment of time, He took upon Himself every hidden,
intentional, unintentional, and presumptuous sin ever
committed. In His gruesome and heart-rending death, He made
provision to heal and reverse all the ravages from our sins.

Having paid for the damage brought by our sins, Jesus
has made a way of liberation and freedom, so we can walk
in true peace and abounding joy. Brothers and sisters, Jesus
fulfilled all the Levitical sacrifices at the high cost of His
very own blood. Bearing our shame and guilt, He became
our perfect trespass offering.

Are you still suffering the devastating effects of sin's
consequences? Although some of that is simply a product
of living in a fallen world, we often overlook the healing
balm Jesus offers. He beckons us to come to Him and
receive healing for our sin-damaged lives.

thirteen

A LIVING SACRIFICE, HOLY AND ACCEPTABLE

So far in our journey, we have seen Jesus as our perfect sacrifice, fulfilling the Levitical offerings in every single detail. We have seen the high cost of His love for us, and how His sacrifice can bring peace and liberty to us today. But how are we supposed to respond to this amazing, sacrificial grace?

In Romans 12:1, the apostle Paul writes an admonishment to us about the choices we should make in response to the great mercy God has shown to us in Christ: *"I beseech you therefore, brethren, by the mercies of God, that you present your bodies a living sacrifice, holy, acceptable to God, which is your reasonable service."*

In practical terms, this means we each need to choose a lifestyle that is a holy sacrifice unto God. This requires laying down our lives and allowing Jesus, the ultimate sacrifice, to express His great love through us to a needy world.

The kind of sacrificial life Paul describes is only possible as we grow in our personal relationship with Christ. In that relationship, we choose to offer our minds, our thoughts, our wills, our emotions, and our actions to the One who loved us so much that He purchased us with His own blood. Seeing that Jesus paid so dear a price to give us eternal life, is it not "reasonable," as Romans 12:1 says, for us to live in radical devotion to Him?

However, some of the terms Paul uses here are rather mind-boggling. What does it mean to be "holy"? What kind of sacrifice is truly "acceptable"? And, in view of the fact that the animals sacrificed in Leviticus always *died*, what could it possibly mean to offer ourselves as "*living* sacrifices"?

Holiness is often misunderstood. True holiness is not a legalistic set of religious rules, but rather a full surrender of our hearts to God. It is a life of relationship and fellowship with Him, characterized by a desire to walk in simple obedience to His ways, whether we understand them or not. In Psalm 40:6-8, David beautifully illustrates what this kind of life looks like:

> *Sacrifice and offering You did not desire; my ears You have opened. Burnt offering and sin offering You did not require. Then I said, "Behold, I come; in the scroll of the book it is written of me. I delight to do Your will, O my God, and Your law is within my heart."*

God desires a heart that DELIGHTS to do His will! He wants His Word to be so engraved in our hearts that holiness is no longer a matter of outward conformity, but rather a response of love. From hearts of gratitude, His image will radiate from our lives. Let us never forget: Religious obligations and rituals cannot produce genuine holiness— only relationship and intimacy can. Christ-likeness is born from that relationship, when our passion for Him is greater than our passion for anything else.

ACCEPTABLE TO GOD?

So how do we know that such a life is truly "acceptable"

to God? David, who still lived under the Levitical sacrificial system, was able to discover something that pleased the Lord far more than animal sacrifices:

> *For you do not desire sacrifice, or else I would give it; You do not delight in burnt offering.* ***The sacrifices of God are a broken spirit, a broken and a contrite heart—these, O God, You will not despise*** (Psalm 51:16-17).

> ***I will praise the name of God*** *with a song, and will magnify Him with thanksgiving.* ***This also shall please the*** LORD ***better than an ox or bull,*** *which has horns and hooves* (Psalm 69:30-31).

These and other verses make it abundantly clear that, above all else, the Lord wants our *hearts*. We can offer up other things as tokens of our devoted hearts, but David realized the emptiness of any outward religious ritual that did not, of first importance, involve the heart.

Once the Lord has captured our hearts, there will no doubt be a transformation of our outward lives as well. Micah 6:8 says it well: *"He has shown you, O man, what is good; and what does the* LORD *require of you but to do justly, to love mercy, and to walk humbly with your God?"* Those who walk humbly with their God will exemplify a life of fairness and mercy toward others.

Each day we are confronted with choices: where we go, what we read, what we listen to, what we watch, what we do. Either we will offer ourselves as living sacrifices, holy and acceptable, or else we will settle for something less. An acceptable sacrifice is a totally surrendered sacrifice, a life that is worthy of the One who gave Himself for us. God's heart for us is that we would receive His abounding grace to overcome the works of the flesh and walk in the fullness of His love.

We obviously are not perfect in ourselves, but that is not the issue. The purifying fire of Jesus, the perfect sacrifice, consumes those who offer themselves as living sacrifices on the altar of obedient surrender. It is impossible to be an "acceptable" sacrifice when we willfully walk in the lusts of the flesh and the pride of life. May we wholeheartedly offer ourselves before the mercy seat of God, allowing Him to remove all bitterness, resentment, cynicism, and lust.

The Lord Jesus, our perfect living sacrifice, longs for communion with us. Are we pursuing His holiness and peace? Do we treasure His Word for us? Do we long for His presence, or do we merely come to Him in religious ritual and formality? Oh, what an honor to be in a living relationship with the King of Kings and the Lord of Lords!

A New Covenant

Let us be clear on this: As Jesus perfectly fulfilled the Old Testament sacrifices, He did more than just confirm the Levitical code. He went far beyond that, inaugurating a wonderful new covenant. Hebrews 8:1-2 explains:

> *Now this is the main point of the things we are saying: We have such a High Priest, who is seated at the right hand of the throne of the Majesty in the heavens, a Minister of the sanctuary and the true tabernacle which the Lord erected, and not man.*

Not only was Jesus prefigured in animals or grain of the Levitical sacrifices, but the high priest of those sacrifices was also a foreshadow of Jesus' later role as the High Priest of a new covenant.

Hebrews gives many reasons why the new covenant is far superior to the old one, proclaiming that Jesus became the *"Mediator of a better covenant, which was established on better promises"* (Hebrews 8:6). First of all, the new covenant is clearly served by a better priesthood. While the Old Testament priests *were prevented by death from continuing*" (Hebrews 7:23), Jesus is a High Priest who lives forever: *"Therefore He is also able to save to the uttermost those who come to God through Him, since He **always lives** to make intercession for them"* (Hebrews 7:25). We can know for certain that our Redeemer and High Priest lives today!

Also, the priests under the Levitical system had to first offer a sacrifice for *themselves* before they could be considered "clean" enough to offer sacrifices for the sins of the people. Again, there is quite a contrast with our new covenant High Priest, Jesus:

> *For such a High Priest was fitting for us, who is holy, harmless, undefiled, separate from sinners, and has become higher than the heavens; who does not need daily, as those high priests, to offer up sacrifices, first for His own sins and then for the people's ...* (Hebrews 7:26-27a).

We have a High Priest who is entirely without sin, with no need to offer sacrifices for his own transgressions.

Another major difference between the old and new covenants has to do with the duration of a sacrifice's efficacy. Under the old covenant, the sacrifices had to continue daily, for there was no permanent atonement for the people's sins. In contrast, when Jesus offered Himself as the perfect sacrifice, He cried out in triumph, *"IT IS **FINISHED!**"* (John 19:30) Hebrews 7:27 notes, *"...He did this **once for all** when He offered up Himself."*

In testimony of the finished work of Jesus on the cross, He did something the old covenant high priests were never able to do: He sat down! Hebrews 1:3 points out this awesome truth: *"...when He had by Himself purged our sins, **sat down** at the right hand of the Majesty on high ..."* (also see Hebrews 10:11-14). His work was finished, and He rested. We can take great comfort in this fact! Our sins have forever been purged by Jesus' death on the cross.

Hebrews 7:7-13 quotes Jeremiah 31-34 to offer some final evidence of the new covenant's superiority over the old:

> For this is the covenant that I will make with the house of Israel after those days, says the LORD: **I will put My laws in their mind and write them on their hearts**; and I will be their God, and they shall be My people. None of them shall teach his neighbor, and none his brother, saying, 'Know the LORD,' for **all shall know Me**, from the least of them to the greatest of them. For I will be merciful to their unrighteousness, and their sins and their lawless deeds I will remember no more.

Under the old covenant, the law was something external written on tablets of stone. But God promises something far better in the new covenant: His laws will be placed inside of us, written on our minds and hearts. Instead of telling us to just try and live up to a legalistic code of external rules, God offers to change our hearts.

The ritualistic offerings of the old covenant guaranteed nothing concerning the hearts of the ones who were coming to the temple to offer sacrifices. However, under the new covenant, we are "born again"—given new hearts and new identities. This results in obedience born out of love instead of legalism.

EMBRACING THE REAL THING

When we begin to comprehend the depth of what transpired on the cross of Calvary 2000 years ago, it sends shivers up and down our spines! The old covenant was a mere shadow of the new, a rough copy of the heavenly realm. The new covenant is more than a foreshadow—it's *the real thing!* The old covenant shadow could not change the heart, nor could it offer everlasting life or even the power to live victoriously in this present life. The new covenant, on the other hand, comes to us *"according to the power of an endless life"* (Hebrews 7:16).

When Jesus hung on the cross as a living sacrifice, He was proclaiming to the universe that the entire law and all Messianic prophecies were fulfilled through Him. He was declaring that death, hell, and the grave were about to be swallowed up in victorious life. This was a declaration of VICTORY, not defeat (1 Corinthians 15:51-58), of joy and not of sadness (Hebrews 12:2). When the Levitical sacrifices came to an end in Him, Jesus literally became our everything: *"... for in Him we live and move and have our being ..."* (Acts. 17:28).

At one moment in time, Jesus—God in the flesh—made the complexity of the old covenant totally simple in Himself. Unfortunately, we in the church today are often not living in that revelation. We have returned to the rituals and lip-service—the shadows instead of the real thing.

Instead of embracing the reality of Christ and His fantastic work for us on the cross, we have often settled for "compensatory facades" (compensating on the outside for a lack or emptiness on the inside). The late Dr. Edwin Louis Cole liked to call this "high gloss, cheap merchandise."

But there is good news. We no longer need to cling to the "shadow of things to come"—*the real thing is here!* Jesus Himself offers to come right where you are today, making Himself real to you in a greater way than you have ever dreamed. The fulfillment of everything you've ever wanted or needed in life can be found in Him!

fourteen

THE GREAT EXCHANGE

Perhaps you are still asking yourself: Is what Jesus did on the cross 2,000 years ago really pertinent to me today? Many professing Christians evidence little excitement or appreciation for the work of Christ on the cross. If you could place a hidden camcorder in most churches, you would see lots of yawns on most Sundays!

It is impossible to have a strong foundation as a Christian unless we have a clear revelation of the passion of Christ and how it can transform our lives today. Without that understanding, we will be apathetic believers at best. I like the question the late Leonard Ravenhill used to put on all of his notes and cards: "Are the things you are living for worth Christ dying for?" This is still a watershed issue that should challenge our values today.

Brother Ravenhill lived what he preached. I remember a time when my left leg was in severe pain from sciatica. I could barely walk, and I was also feeling a lot of emotional pressure at that time in my life. My nerves were increasingly becoming frayed as I tossed and turned at night, unable to sleep. During this stressful period, I got a little handwritten letter from Brother Ravenhill:

> *If God wills, we will come to Houston one day. Presently, dear Martha and I are recovering from a tough attack of flu. Then the sciatic nerve in my left leg struck a painful blow. Now I have a limp, but so had Jacob, and it does not seem I shall travel much this year. But with the Psalmist we say, 'My times are in Thy hands,' ready to stay ready for my place to fill, ready for service, lowly or great, ready to do His will.*

At that time, Brother Ravenhill was not only battling the flu and sciatica, he was also in his 80s and had suffered four major heart attacks. And here I was, in my mid-30s at the time, complaining about my health and having an old-fashioned pity party.

Upon reading Brother Ravenhill's letter, I couldn't help but think, *Listen to this guy! If this sciatic thing is bugging me, it must be terrible for him. But all he can think about is serving God!* His letter ended with this: "He is no fool who exchanges his burden of sin for the burden of the Lord."

Brother Ravenhill had all kinds of phrases that seemed to leap right up and hit me square between the eyes. This one was certainly no exception. As I began to meditate upon his attitude during a stressful time in his life, I was convicted of my own self-centered murmuring. But I was also greatly encouraged in handing my own "burden" before the Lord, despite the way I was feeling.

As I continued to meditate on Brother Ravenhill's concluding statement about the exchange of the burden of sin for the burden of the Lord, I began to see how Jesus exchanged our filthy rags for His robes of righteousness. We studied earlier the old hymn that says, "We owed a debt we could not pay; He paid a debt He did not owe." Yes, He exchanged His own life and holiness for the debt of sin which we could not pay. He willingly experienced our sin, our hell, and our separation so we could be brought into loving fellowship with the Father.

THE EXCHANGE OF BURDENS

The first exchange Jesus made on our behalf was to give us eternal life in exchange for our sentence of hell and eternal death. But the exchange doesn't end there. We should be willing, as Brother Ravenhill said, to exchange our burden of sin for the burden of the Lord. By that I mean we should cultivate a burden to do the will of God, whatever the cost.

Although this could be manifested in a variety of ways, in many cases it will mean reaching out to hurting, broken, and lost people. But whatever the Lord's burden is for our lives, that is what we should be willing to embrace in exchange for our sins. If our sins have been cleansed yet we have no passion to follow the Lord's heart for our lives, something is seriously wrong!

When we exchanged our filthy rags for His perfect righteousness, we made a commitment to the Lord. In that commitment we said, "Not my will, but your will be done. I no longer belong to myself. You have bought me with a price, and that price was your very own blood." Paul challenged the Corinthians on this very matter:

> *Or do you not know that your body is the temple of the Holy Spirit who is in you, whom you have from God, and you are not your own? For you were bought at a price; therefore glorify God in your body and in your spirit, which are God's* (1 Corinthians 6:19-20).

Paul seemed to be wondering if the Corinthians had forgotten this foundation stone of a fruitful Christian life. Christianity is not living any way you want, with a quick call to Jesus for help whenever you get yourself in trouble. The life of faith is not a "pick and choose" game where we keep what we like and discard what we don't. Christianity is not making the Word of God fit what we want so we can continue to satisfy our own fleshly desires and greed. Our quest should be to fit into God's plans rather than trying to squeeze Him into ours.

When we die to ourselves and commit ourselves to the full lordship of Jesus, our hearts become less likely to be drawn into deception. As Jesus promises in John 7:17, *"If anyone wills to do His will, he shall know concerning the doctrine, whether it is from God or whether I speak of My own authority."* Thus, a firm commitment to do the will of God will keep us from falling into error by entertaining what is *not* His will for our lives. When we are not focused on God's covenant for our lives, it is so easy to become deceived through vain imaginations, the lust of the eye, the lust of the flesh, and the pride of life.

We need to orientate our minds toward identifying with our new life in Christ instead of our old man, who was dead in trespasses and sins. When we identify with our pasts, it is impossible to break the strongholds of sin in our lives. This "identification" problem stands at the core of most struggling Christians.

Despite the fact that Jesus died to give us new life through His resurrection, we are busy thinking about and doing things which amount to resurrecting the "old man"! So it becomes very easy to get off into error when we don't totally die at the cross with Christ.

THE 'LEPROSY' OF SIN

Leviticus 14:1-4 describes the "great exchange" in a truly wonderful way:

Then the LORD spoke to Moses, saying, "This shall be the law of the leper for the day of his cleansing: He shall be brought to the priest. And the priest shall go out of the camp, and the priest shall examine him; and indeed, if the leprosy is healed in the leper, then the priest shall command to take for him who is to be cleansed two living and clean birds, cedar wood, scarlet, and hyssop."

Leprosy, in the Bible, is symbolic of the uncleanness of sin and especially the result of sin: death. Aside from a miracle, there was no cure for leprosy. (Yet, God provided instructions for those who would be cured! Proof that He wants to do miracles!) Because it was highly contagious, those who were infected had to live in separate colonies. If you were a leper and someone approached you on the road, by law you had to raise your arms and shout, "Unclean, unclean!" so people would know to avoid you for fear of being infected.

God uses leprosy in Leviticus 14 to illustrate how our sins were cleansed in Jesus 2000 years ago on the cross. This is the same chapter Jesus referred to in Matthew 8:1-4 after He healed a leper. When the leper was "cleansed" or healed, Jesus told him to follow the prescription in Leviticus 14. A healed leper would undergo a specific ritual designed to teach about the Messiah and His redemptive work.

Leviticus 14 is loaded with symbolic references that are easy to miss. "Cedar wood" is representative of the wood of the cross, and thus becomes a symbol of the crucifixion. "Scarlet" is a type of the blood of Christ which was shed on that cross for our sakes. "Hyssop" is symbolic of the purging Jesus experienced on our behalf (Psalm 51:7, Hebrews 1:3), cleansing away the sins of the world by His blood.

The chapter continues:

> *And the priest shall command that one of the birds be killed in an earthen vessel over running water. And for the living bird, he shall take it, the cedar wood and the scarlet and the hyssop, and dip them and the living bird in the blood of the bird that was killed over the running water. And he shall sprinkle it seven times on him who is to be cleansed from the leprosy, and shall pronounce him clean, and shall let the living bird loose in the open field* (Leviticus 14:5-7).

What is the significance of the two birds? Actually, they represent the same person, but with a slightly different twist. The first bird is killed in an *earthen* vessel over running water. The first bird typifies God manifested in the "earthen vessel" of flesh—Jesus of Nazareth. "Running water" (sometimes referred to as *living* water) is figurative of the Holy Spirit. Jesus was "killed … over running water" in the sense that, from beginning to end, He was anointed by and saturated with the Holy Spirit "without measure" (see John 1:32, Matthew 26:6-13, John 4:7-14).

The second (living) bird is taken together with the cedar wood, the scarlet, and the hyssop, and dipped in the blood of the bird that was killed over running water. The leper is sprinkled with this blood seven times, then the living bird is loosed into the open field.

Many commentators believe the second bird is figurative of us as we are cleansed of our sins, but I believe this is only partially true. In this passage, the sinner is mainly portrayed by the leper who is being cleansed. The second bird, then, must be figurative of Jesus, yet in His *resurrected* form.

Think about it! The "living" bird is taken together with the elements representative of the crucifixion. It is dipped in the "sinless" blood of the bird which was killed over running water, then let loose into the open field after the leper is sprinkled with blood seven times.

Jesus overcame the world *"by water and blood"* (1 John 5:5-6). Although He was crucified, death could not hold Him because of His sinless blood. He was resurrected from the dead by the living water of the Holy Spirit. Then He sprinkled His blood before the temple in heaven, once and for all, so that He could forever cleanse all those who would come to Him (John 20:17, Hebrews 9:12).

So the second (living) bird is first and foremost the resurrected Christ. Second, it represents all of those who place themselves *in* Him through faith. In turn, we are set free from sin into the open field of His love. The second and *living* bird, figurative of the resurrection life of Jesus, is what actually cleanses the "leper" (you and me) from sin!

In the picture of these two birds, we see the great exchange that took place 2000 years ago on Calvary. Through His shed blood, Jesus exchanged His eternal life for our sins. He was the "bird" killed on our behalf that, in Him, we might fly away in perfect freedom. And in Him we become the living bird—alive because we were "dipped" (and washed) in His blood. Our filthy rags were exchanged for His robes of righteousness. Not only did He buy us with a price, He also came to live within us as the Holy Spirit.

In light of such awesome redemptive love, how can we not give ourselves totally and irrevocably to Him? Our foremost desire should be to honor God and gladly identify with Jesus instead of being ashamed of Him. For this reason, Hebrews 10:29 teaches us that we trample on the blood of Christ when we choose to identify with our old man of sin rather than with our new man who was created in righteousness, in Him.

Leviticus 14:8-11 provides a beautiful picture of a sinner (leper), who is cleansed and presented blameless before the Lord and the entire congregation. Then, in verses 12-14, we see a teaching that instructs us how to walk in our "cleanness" and live out the new life we have been given:

> *And the priest shall take one male lamb and offer it as a trespass offering, and the log of oil, and wave them as a wave offering before the LORD. Then he shall kill the lamb in the place where he kills the sin offering and the burnt offering, in a holy place; for as the sin offering is the priest's, so is the trespass offering. It is most holy. The priest shall take some of the blood of the trespass offering,* **and the priest shall put it on the tip of the right ear of him who is to be cleansed, on the thumb of his right hand, and on the big toe of his right foot.**

The heart of the teaching here lies in verse 14. The blood of the trespass offering is placed upon the tip of the **right ear**, the **right thumb,** and the **big toe** of the right foot. Now what does this possibly mean to us? The bottom line is that, through Jesus, God has provided the way for us to live a life of consecration and holiness. The blood applied to these three specific areas of the body depicts the sanctifying element of the blood of Jesus.

"Sanctify" means "to set apart for a specific use" or "to make holy." Therefore, the blood applied to the tip of the right ear teaches that our ears are to be set apart for His use. They are consecrated to be supernaturally "tuned in" to the voice of Jesus, our Good Shepherd: *"My sheep hear My voice, and I know them, and they follow Me"* (John 10:27).

As vessels set apart in honor of the King, we have a responsibility to guard what enters our hearts and minds. If we allow our temples to be defiled by the filth of the world— which is so prevalent in television, magazines, and music today—we dishonor our Father and inhibit the work He desires to do through our lives. May our ears and eyes be sanctified for His purposes!

The "right hand" or "right arm" in Scripture is figurative of *action*. It speaks of doing something or accomplishing some type of work (Psalm 90:17, Acts 13:17). Our "works" have the potential to be good or bad, righteous or unrighteous, meaningful or meaningless. Applying the blood of our trespass offering to the right hand is a further act of consecration. God is consecrating our deeds, all that we do in His name.

If we sin and seek forgiveness through our trespass offering, God desires that we consecrate our future deeds in that area of our lives. Anything we set our hands to do— whether in business, ministry, or other areas of life—should glorify God! *"... whatever you do,"* Paul told the Corinthians, *"do all to the glory of God"* (1 Corinthians 10:31).

Last of all, the big toe is mentioned because of its unique role as part of the entire foot. The spiritual parallel is obvious. We *walk* with our foot. The big toe has the primary role of bringing *balance* to each and every step that we take. Without a big toe, it is nearly impossible to maintain an even keel. In fact, if you were to cut off your big toes, you would probably have trouble standing up straight, much less trying to walk without falling over. We trip ourselves up spiritually when we choose to go places and do things that are not godly.

The blood of the trespass offering applied to the "big toe of the right foot" is a message from the Lord that our steps should be led by *Him*. Setting apart our steps to walk in God's purposes, we are called to *"keep in step with the Spirit"* (Galatians 5:25 NIV). Everywhere we set our feet should be considered holy ground for the King (Joshua 1:3).

Let us commit ourselves to walking courageously and unashamedly in this fallen world, bringing the love and presence of God with us! As Paul reminded the Corinthians, we are called to diffuse *"the fragrance of His knowledge in every place"* (2 Corinthians 2:14).

The picture is clear: Through the blood of Jesus, our entire lives—whatever we hear, speak, think, or do—should be consecrated to the glory of God. This is not just a matter of human effort to attain holiness. Rather, it is the Holy Spirit who sanctifies us, setting us apart for His use (2 Thessalonians 2:13, Philippians 2:13, Romans 15:16). This is exactly what is happening in Leviticus 14:15-17, where the "oil" represents the anointing of the Holy Spirit:

> *And the priest shall take some of the log of oil, and pour it into the palm of his own left hand. Then the priest shall dip his right finger in the oil that is in his left hand, and shall sprinkle some of the oil with his finger seven times before the* Lord. *And the rest of the oil in his hand, the priest shall put some on the tip of the right ear of him who is to be cleansed, on the thumb of his right hand, and on the big toe of his right foot, on the blood of the trespass offering.*

The anointing oil, representative of the Holy Spirit, is applied on the right ear, right thumb, and big toe of the right foot. What is God saying here? When we allow Jesus to apply His blood to our lives, washing away our sins, we also consent to consecrate our lives to Him. At this point, the Holy Spirit comes into our hearts and *seals* the work of the cross in our hearts and lives (Ephesians 1:3-14, especially verse 13). That is why the oil is placed *on top of* the blood of the trespass offering in these three special places. The blood is the foundation of our anointing by the Holy Spirit.

SEALED, SANCTIFIED, AND EMPOWERED

After *sealing* the work of salvation in our lives, the Holy Spirit then sets out to *sanctify* our lives as we determine to walk with Him. Day by day, the sanctifying presence of the Spirit convicts us of sin and leads us to repentance. He is continually speaking to our hearts, saying, "This is the way; walk in it."

Another profound truth is contained in Leviticus 14:18:

> *The rest of the oil that is in the priest's hand he shall put on the head of him who is to be cleansed. So the priest shall make atonement for him before the Lord.*

What is God teaching in this verse? What is represented by pouring the "rest" (remnant) of the oil on the head of the person who was to be cleansed? The Holy Spirit has not only come to *seal* and *sanctify* us, but He also came to *empower us* for the work God has called us to do (Micah 3:8, Acts 1:8, Acts 2:1-4).

Without His power, we can do nothing (John 15:5, Zechariah 4:6). The Holy Spirit has come to bear witness to the words and life of Jesus in great and mighty ways (Acts 4:31-33). This is an Old Testament foreshadow of the baptism in the Holy Spirit. Just as the "remnant" of the log of oil was poured upon the leper who was cleansed, so is the Holy Spirit poured out on all of those who determine to obey and follow Him. In the book of Acts, the Holy Spirit is described as coming *upon* the believers in their baptism, or as *filling* them to overflowing.

Observing the progression of the leper's healing, we can learn a lot about the process of salvation in our lives. The leper first had to be cleansed and sealed, as do we. He then was sanctified, set apart for God's purposes. Finally, the leper needed to be empowered by the anointing oil of the Spirit. When we receive the baptism of the Holy Spirit, we are committing ourselves to receiving *all* of God's plan and commission for our lives. God makes provision for all of this in Leviticus 14!

This must be more than a doctrine or theory! We need to receive *power* to serve Him. This includes power to go out with supernatural signs, wonders, and miracles, bearing witness to the living reality of Jesus. Our Savior is *alive,* and this is the central difference between our God and the "gods" of other faiths.

It is said that *"with **great power** the apostles gave witness to the **resurrection** of the Lord Jesus"* (Acts 4:33). The core message of the early church was the *resurrection* of Jesus, not just His crucifixion. Today, as then, this message must be preached in the power of the Spirit.

How do we receive this power? Acts 5:32 states quite simply that the Holy Spirit is given to those who *obey* Him. We can simply follow Jesus and let Him worry about the manifestation of His power in our lives. All things are possible to those who *believe* (Mark 9:23). The old hymn sums it up very well, "Trust [i.e., believe] and obey, for there's no other way, to be happy in Jesus, but to trust and obey." As we set our hearts to believe and obey the Lord, His power and blessing will be released in our lives.

So what about you? Is your life surrendered and set apart to God? Or do you still carry around the guilt and shame of your past? Are you walking around in defeat and fear, ashamed of what your life has come to? It's time for us to lay our lives down before the Lord! We need to truly make Him Lord of our lives, exchanging our "filthy rags" for His beautiful robes of righteousness.

We need to let Him speak to us clearly as to the direction our lives should go. Let's kneel and say to Him, "Not my will, Lord, but Your will be done. Transform my life and help me be disciplined as to what I allow into my mind and my heart. Let me honor You in all my ways, so I can hold my head high and say, 'I am not ashamed of the Gospel of Jesus Christ!'"

Be assured, this is a prayer the Lord will honor if it is prayed with a sincere heart. Jesus died to make this great exchange, and He rose again to give it *life*. How can anyone refuse an offer like this? Jesus beckons us to follow Him into a life of expectancy and joy!

fifteen

MISSION ACCOMPLISHED!

A very important event occurred at the end of Jesus' time on the cross:

> *And Jesus cried out again with a loud voice, and yielded up His spirit. Then, behold, the veil of the temple was torn in two from top to bottom; and the earth quaked, and the rocks were split (Matthew 27:50-51).*

At the very moment Jesus cried out with a loud voice, *"It is finished ... Father, into Your hands I commit My spirit"* (John 19:30, Luke 23:46), the veil in the temple ripped from top to bottom.

This was no mean feat! The veil was of considerable size and weight. It is estimated that the veil was about 30 feet wide and 90 feet high, so large and weighty that it had to be supported by four pillars. So when we read that the veil was torn from top to bottom, please understand that a supernatural event is being described, as if some giant pair of hands took the veil and tore it as if it were nothing. We are looking at nothing less than the hands of God reaching down to rip away that which separated us from His presence!

This veil in the temple separated the Holy Place from the *Most* Holy Place or Holy of Holies. During the days of the tabernacle, the Holy of Holies contained the Ark of the Covenant, which was the manifestation of the presence of God. Because the holiness of God would not allow the presence of sinful flesh before Him, no one was allowed to go behind the veil into the presence of God except for once a year, when the high priest was allowed to go into the Holy of Holies in order to make atonement for Israel. This was on the Day of Atonement.

In the days of the tabernacle, all Israel held their breath as the blood of the lamb was taken before the mercy seat of the ark. If the priest was not right with God or if he had not properly executed the sacrifice, he would be struck dead on the spot for going inside the veil without his sins being properly "covered." So all Israel waited breathlessly to hear the tinkling of the little bells on the fringe of his robe as he walked back through the veil. Can you imagine the mounting suspense? If all was well, I can just see the high priest coming out and raising his hands with joy, saying, "Praise the Lord, the sacrifice for sins has been accepted!"

Again, Jesus remarkably fulfilled this ceremony ministered by the high priest during the Day of Atonement. When Jesus, the High Priest of the new covenant, finished His work on the cross 2000 years ago, He shouted, "T-E-T-E-L-E-S-T-A-I-!," which means "It is finished!" in Greek. His sacrifice was not only "acceptable," it was so perfect and powerful that it ripped away the veil of the temple, giving *all of us* access to the presence of God through faith. "T-E-T-E-L-E-S-T-A-I-!" was more than an acknowledgment of death as He felt His life fading away. It was a shout of *victory!* In other ancient manuscripts, the word was sometimes translated "paid in full." He was saying, "I've done it! My mission is accomplished! The veil is taken away, and all can come boldly before the Father in My name!" (Ephesians 2:18, 3:12)

REJOICE AND DRAW NEAR!

Christians, it is time to quit struggling. Jesus already accomplished the hard part on the cross, and now He wants to apply that work to our own hearts. As Ephesians 2:14-15 tells us, He wants to be our peace. He *"has broken down the middle wall of separation, having abolished in His flesh the enmity, that is, the law of commandments contained in ordinances ... "*

What did Jesus do about all the laws, commandments, and traditions which were designed to bring us into the presence of God, but *couldn't* because of our sinful natures? He put them to death in His own flesh by fulfilling them all perfectly for us.

If Jesus had just lived and died for us, it would have meant very little. However, He also rose from the dead so that He might give us *power* to do that which is pleasing to God. He gives us that power by dwelling within us as the Holy Spirit, living through us as we choose to surrender to Him. That is why grace is not an excuse to sin. Grace goes beyond a grant of pardon. It is first and foremost the enabling power of our holy God, who lives within us.

Jesus never pulled back from His mission, nor should we shrink from ours. In His dying breath, His heart must have been shouting, "Come on! Follow me with all your heart! Your life has meaning to me, and I have a fantastic plan for you. You've got purpose now. Embrace Me, and let's walk boldly into the future together."

Hebrews 10:19-25 captures the spirit of His great victory as well as our invitation to respond:

Therefore, brethren, having boldness to enter the Holiest by the blood of Jesus, by a new and living way which He consecrated for us, through the veil, that is, His flesh, and having a High Priest over the house of God, let us draw near with a true heart in full assurance of faith, having our hearts sprinkled from an evil conscience and our bodies washed with pure water. Let us hold fast the confession of our hope without wavering, for He who promised is faithful. And let us consider one another in order to stir up love and good works, not forsaking the assembling of ourselves together, as is the manner of some, but exhorting one another, and so much the more as you see the Day approaching.

This passage says it all, doesn't it? Let's not waiver in our faith anymore! Whatever we do, let's do it with a pure conscience, stirring up each other to love and good works. Let's keep our eyes on our eternal reward and the day when we'll enjoy eternal fellowship with Him in His Kingdom.

THE MISSION STILL AHEAD

Although Jesus' mission was fully completed on the cross, our mission is still in progress. Will we fulfill the mission He has set before us? Will He be able to one day tell us, *"Well done, good and faithful servant ... Enter into the joy of your Lord"*? (Matthew 25:23)

When we willingly lay down our rights and fully surrender to God, there is not defeat but victory. When the world sees us laying down our own desires and plans out of love for God, they will be struck by the character of Jesus reflected in us. They will see His peace and presence on our countenances, and this will draw them "through the veil" into intimate relationship with God. This, my brothers and sisters, is what true Christianity is all about!

Is Jesus presently accomplishing His mission in your life? Or do you allow unbelief, guilt, frustration, or fear to choke out His purposes for you? Say "yes" to Jesus, and give a shout of victory in your life. Understand that nothing you go through—nothing!—will ever be able to separate you from the love of God (Romans 8:28-39).

With great and tender love, Jesus is watching passionately over all whose hearts are sincerely seeking Him (2 Chronicles 16:9a). Follow Him! He is the Way, the Truth, and the Life. No one can come to the Father except through Him, but He has made a way for YOU through His work on the cross (John 14:6).

"I simply argue that the cross should be raised in the center of the marketplace as well as on the steeple of the church. I am recovering the claim that Jesus was not crucified between two candles, but on a cross between two thieves; on the town's garbage heap; at a crossroads, so cosmopolitan they had to write his title in Hebrew, in Latin, and in Greek. At the kind of place where cynics talk smut, and thieves curse, and soldiers gamble. Because that is where He died. That is what He died for. And that is what He died about. And that is where church people ought to be, and what church people ought to be about."

George MacLeod (1895-1991)
famous Scottish preacher

About the Author

Dr. J. Doug Stringer is the founder and president of Turning Point Ministries International, which birthed an international movement known as Somebody Cares, a network of organizations impacting their communities through unified grassroots efforts. Doug began identifying community needs through his work in the inner-city of Houston, Texas in 1981. The collaborative network has grown rapidly and now impacts cities around the world.

A licensed pastoral counselor and ordained minister, Doug holds a Ph. D. in leadership and human development. He is recognized for his contributions in both secular and sacred arenas. Doug received congressional recognition for the work of Somebody Cares in 2001 and the Barbara Jordan Leadership Award in 1995. He has served with the Houston area Council on Gangs and as a Community Relations Consultant for Houston Police Department's Community Outreach Division and currently serves on HPD's Youth Police Advisory Council. Doug is the co-founder of Global Compassion Network (GCN), a network of worldwide compassion ministries, and serves as a board member or advisor for a variety of organizations, including: Asian Task Force, World Blessing Foundation, Sentinel Group with George Otis Jr., Mission Houston, Mission America and Youth-Reach Houston. He was also appointed by the Governor of Texas to the board of the One Star Foundation.

Somebody Cares has implemented several citywide strategies now multiplied in cities across the nation including a mentoring program for youth known as Youth Guidance Consultants. Somebody Cares developed an anti-gang and at-risk youth intervention handbook, which is utilized by the Police Department. An annual back-to-school youth outreach called X-Day at the Bay and benevolent aid during the holiday season known as Holiday of Hope and other outreaches were integral parts of Somebody Cares' efforts over the years. In addition, Somebody Cares has provided awareness and training for potential adoptive parents known as Hope in Houston.

Doug is the author of the books *It's Time to Cross the Jordan*, *The Fatherless Generation* and *Somebody Cares*, and is currently working on several new projects including *Living Life Well* and *Who's Your Daddy Now?* He is published in numerous magazines and websites including: *The Houston Chronicle, New Man, Charisma, Decision Magazine, National Religious Broadcasters Magazine, Christian Single* and www.crosswalk.com. Doug is a frequent presenter at workshops such as "Save Our Children," "Seminar of Youth Problems," and "A Forum on Racial & Ethnic Tensions in Schools," as well as Cultural Awareness forums. He is also a sought after speaker at religious, political, educational and civic gatherings.

As an Asian-American, Doug is considered a bridge-builder and ambassador of reconciliation amongst various ethnic and religious groups. From police departments and congressmen, to international government officials, Doug shares a key concept: Working together, we can be more effective in our community efforts.

For more information you may call (713) 621-1498, fax (713) 621-2076, or visit www.dougstringer.com.